Functional Programming in JavaScript

Cristian Salcescu

Functional Programming in JavaScript

Functional Programming in JavaScript

Cristian Salcescu

Copyright © 2020 Cristian Salcescu

ISBN-13: 979-8671513851

History:

August 2020 First Edition

February 2022 Revision

Contents

Introduction	9
Setup	11
Chapter 01: Primitives	**15**
Primitives	15
Methods on Primitives	16
Immutability	17
Variables	17
Recap	18
Chapter 02: Immutable Data Objects	**19**
Objects	19
Immutability	20
Freezing	20
Linting	21
Working with Immutable Objects	22
Recap	23
Chapter 03: Functions	**25**
Function Declarations	25
Function Expressions	26
Arrow Function Expressions	27
Arity	27
Pure Functions	27
Recap	28
Chapter 04: Arrays	**29**
Filtering	29
Mapping	31

Aggregating	33
Sorting	35
Searching	36
forEach	37
Impure Operations	38
Changing Arrays	38
Recap	40

Chapter 05: First-Class Functions — 41
First-Class Functions	41
Higher-Order Functions	43
Closures	45
Recap	46

Chapter 06: Statements — 47
Expressions	47
Statement Declaration	48
Conditional Statements	48
Loop Statements	52
Disruptive Statements	53
Recap	55

Chapter 07: Recursion — 57
Recursive Factorial	57
Tail-Call Optimization	59
Stack Overflow Error	59
Trampoline	61
Traversing a Tree	62
Recap	64

Chapter 08: Pipelines and Currying — 65
Pipelines	65
Chaining	66
Currying	69
Reduce Pipeline	70
Recap	71

Chapter 09: Functors — 73
Functors	74
Functor Laws	74
Category Theory	76

Functors in Practice	76
Arrays	78
Recap	79

Chapter 10: Monads — 81
- Flat Mapping 81
- Monads 83
- Monad Laws 83
- Alternative Creation and Naming 85
- Arrays 87
- Recap 89

Chapter 11: Immutable Collections — 91
- List 91
- Map 94
- Recap 96

Chapter 12: Lazy Transformations — 97
- Transducers 97
- Sequence 101
- Range 102
- Recap 105

Chapter 13: Generators — 107
- Finite Generators 107
- toArray 108
- forEach 109
- take 109
- Custom Generators 110
- Recap 111

Chapter 14: Promises — 113
- Creating Promises 114
- Success Handling 114
- Error Handling 116
- Chaining 117
- Asynchronous Operations 118
- Functor Laws 121
- Monad Laws 123
- Recap 125

Chapter 15: Observables — 127
  Creation Operators 127
  Pipeable Operators 130
  Observers 132
  Subscriptions 133
  Higher-Order Observables 134
  Flattening Operators 135
  Combining Observables 138
  Functor Laws 139
  Monad Laws 140
  Recap 141

Chapter 16: Elm Architecture — 143
  Elm Architecture 143
  Counter with Elm 144
  Counter with React and Redux 146
  Random Number with Elm 148
  Random Number with React and Redux 152
  Recap 154

Chapter 17: Functional Paradigm — 155
  Purity 155
  Immutability 158
  Pipelines 159
  Loops 159
  Naming 159
  Final Thoughts 160

Introduction

Functional programming is becoming more popular and this book aims to bring clarity on how to use JavaScript as a functional language.

It turns out that JavaScript has everything it needs to be used as a functional language. We just need to remove features from the language.

In essence, we are going to remove the `this` keyword from our code. That means we are not going to use classes or methods using the `this` keyword. It also implies not using custom prototypes.

Removing `this` has other benefits. `this` is the source of much confusion in JavaScript, mainly because it depends on how the function is invoked, not where the function is defined. There are many situations where `this` points to an unexpected function context and that leads to bugs. By removing `this` all the related problems are gone.

JavaScript is both a functional programming language and a prototype-based language. If we get rid of `this`, we are left with JavaScript as a functional programming language. That is even better.

That being said, we can remove `this` from our code by enabling linting.

Here is an example of a lint configuration file disabling the `this` keyword from an application built with Create React App.

```
{
  "extends": ["react-app"],
  "plugins": [
      "immutable"
  ],
  "rules": {
      "immutable/no-this": "error"
  }
}
```

JavaScript without `this` looks like a better functional programming language.

Source Code

The project files from this book are available at https://github.com/cristisalcescu/functional-programming-in-javascript.

Feedback

I will be glad to hear your feedback. For comments, questions, or suggestions regarding this book send me an email to cristisalcescu@gmail.com. Thanks in advance for considering to write a review of the book.

Setup

First, we need to setup our development environment to use the latest JavaScript features.

Package Manager

A package manager is a tool used to track project dependencies in an easy to use manner. At the time of writing, Node.js package manager, in short `npm`, is the most popular. Let's start by installing Node.js.

The following commands can then be used in command prompt to check the Node.js and npm versions:

```
node --version
npm --v
```

NPM Packages

With `npm` we can install additional packages. These packages are the application dependencies.

The `package.json` file stores all the node packages used in the project. These packages are the application dependencies. The application can be shared with other developers without sharing all the node packages. Installing all the packages defined in the `package.json` file can be done using the `npm install` command.

Start by creating a package.json file using `npm`.

```
npm init
```

We need a tool that converts our JavaScript code into a backward-compatible version and has support for modules. We need Babel. Go and install the necessary packages.

```
npm install @babel/core @babel/node @babel/preset-env --save
```

The installed packages can be found in the `node_modules` folder. The `--save` flag tells npm to store the package requirement in the `package.json` file.

In order to use the latest JavaScript, we need to enable a preset. Create the `.babelrc` file and enable the babel/preset-env preset.

```
{
  "presets": ["@babel/preset-env"]
}
```

Linting

Linting is the process of analyzing the code for potential errors and stylistic problems. A linter is a tool that runs and reports these problems. Linters are also useful for code formatting and for using best practices.

We are going to use ES Lint. Start by installing it.

```
npm install eslint --save-dev
```

Lint rules can be defined in a configuration file named `.eslintrc.*`.

Next, set up a configuration file.

```
npx eslint --init
```

One plugin we are going to use is eslint-plugin-functional so let's install it.

```
npm install eslint-plugin-functional --save-dev
```

Now go to the `.eslintrc.json` config file an write the lint rule that forbids the usage of `this` keyword.

```
{
    "plugins": [
        "functional"
    ],
    "rules": {
        "functional/no-this-expression": "error"
    }
}
```

Here is how you can run linting on all files inside the `src` folder.

```
npx eslint src
```

In an application created with Create React App we can force linting before starting the development server by prepending the `npx eslint src` command followed by `&&`.

```
"scripts": {
    "start": "npx eslint src && react-scripts start"
}
```

Using `&&` means that things on both sides of the `&&` must evaluate to `true`. If the command on the left side fails the command on the right side will not execute, so in our case, the development server won't start.

IDE

For code editing, we need an Integrated Development Environment, IDE in short.

I am going to use Visual Studio Code but feel free to use any editor you prefer.

In order to write commands open the application folder in Visual Studio Code. Then open the terminal from Terminal -> New Terminal and execute the command.

To run the code inside the `filter.js` file for example, and check the results, we can just use the following command.

`npx babel-node filter.js`

For instant linting feedback we can install the ESLint extension for VSCode. Linting allows us to work in a better subset of JavaScript.

Chapter 01: Primitives

We start our learning journey by looking at the first kind of values available in the language.

Primitives

The primitive values include numbers, strings, booleans, `null`, and `undefined`. Log some of these primitive values in the console.

```
console.log(1);
console.log('text');
console.log(true);
```

All these primitive values have a type. We can find the type of a value using the `typeof` operator. Check some of them.

```
console.log(typeof(1));
//"number"

console.log(typeof(''));
//"string"

console.log(typeof(true));
//"boolean"
```

There are two number types `Number` and `BigInt`. Mainly we are going to use the first one which stores double-precision floating-point numbers. It is important to know that floating-point arithmetic is not accurate.

```
console.log(0.1 + 0.2);
//0.30000000000000004

console.log(0.1 + 0.2 === 0.3);
```

```
//false
```

The integer arithmetic is accurate up to 15 digits.

```
console.log(1 + 2 === 3);
//true
```

`BigInt` is used to represent larger numbers. We can create such numbers by appending `n` to the end of an integer literal.

```
console.log(12345678987654321n);
```

Strings are texts. There are three ways to define a string value, single quotes, double quotes and backticks.

```
"text"
'text'
`text`
```

Undefined is a type with one value `undefined`. Null is a type with one value `null`. Boolean is a type with two values `true` and `false`.

Methods on Primitives

Primitives are not objects but they seem to behave like objects because they have methods. For example, we can call the `toLowerCase` method on a string primitive. How is that possible if a string is not an object? JavaScript creates a wrapper object and destroys it in order to run the `toLowerCase` method.

```
'TEXT'.toLowerCase();
//"text"
```

We can access existing properties on primitives but we cannot change them or create new ones. For example, the `length` property returns the size of a string.

```
'ABCDEFG'.length
//7

'ABCDEFG'.type = 'letters';
//Cannot create property 'type' on string 'ABCDEFG'
```

The only primitives that are not treated as objects are `null` and `undefined`. Trying to call a method on them will throw an error.

```
null.toString();
//Cannot read property 'toString' of null
```

Immutability

An immutable value is a value that once created cannot be changed.

Primitives are immutable. For example, when using a method on a string we create new value. Here is an example of using the `trim` method that removes whitespace from both sides of a string.

```
' 123 '.trim();
//'123';
```

The `trim` method does not modify the existing string. It creates a new one.

Variables

We need to make a distinction between variables and values. Variables are not values. Variables store values.

We can assign values to variables. At this point, variables hold those values. Variables have a name and we can refer the value using the name of the variable.

We store a value in a variable using the assignment = keyword. Variables can be declared with `let`, `var`, or `const` statements. When we declare a variable without assigning it a value, it has the default value of `undefined`.

```
let x;
console.log(x);
//undefined
```

Values don't contain variables. Values may contain other values.

Values have a type. Variables have the type of the value they store. Variables are not tied to a type. A value always has the same type. `1` is always a number, but the following variable `x` can first by of type number and then on type string.

```
let x;
x = 1;
x = '';
```

When the value stored by the variable changes, the type of the variable may change. Dynamic typing means that the type of the variable can change at run-time. This happens only for variables declared with `let` or `var`.

`const` declares variables that cannot be reassigned so they cannot change their type.

Recap

Numbers, strings, booleans, `null`, and `undefined` are primitive values.

Immutable values cannot be changed once created. Primitive values are immutable.

Values can be stored in variables. Variables infer the type of the value they store.

Chapter 02: Immutable Data Objects

Next, we will look at what objects are and how to create and work with immutable objects.

In functional programming, we are going to use objects as data structures. They will store data and have no behavior.

Objects

Objects are a collection of properties. Each property has a key and a value. Take a look at an object in the console.

```
const book = {
  title : 'JavaScript Allongé'
  author: 'Reginald Braithwaite'
  category: 'JavaScript'
};

console.log(book);
```

The key is a string that is unique in the collection. It is case sensitive.

We can access a property using the dot notation or the bracket notation.

```
console.log(book.title);
//"JavaScript Allongé"

console.log(book["title"]);
```

Immutability

Immutability is one of the core principles of functional programming.

Mutation means change. Saying that we changed an object's property is the same as saying we mutated that object.

An immutable object once created cannot be changed. JavaScript objects are nothing like that. They can be modified. They are not immutable. Consider the next example:

```
let fruit = {
  name: 'Apple'
};

fruit.name = 'Orange'
//{name : 'Orange'}
```

As you notice, we can change the existing `fruit` object. The same thing happens even when we use the `const` keyword declaration.

```
const fruit = {
  name: 'Apple'
};

fruit.name = 'Orange'
// {name : 'Orange'}
```

The `const` keyword refers to the variable, not to the value it stores. It means the variable cannot be reassigned. It truly becomes a constant when the value it stores is immutable.

Freezing

I order to create an immutable object we can freeze it at creation.

```
const fruit = Object.freeze({
 name: 'Apple'
});

fruit.name = 'Orange'
// Cannot assign to read only property 'name' of object
```

The only limitation is that `Object.freeze` does shallow freezing. It affects the immediate properties of the object, the ones at the first level in the tree. If for example one of these properties contains another object, that object will not be affected. Look at the next example.

```
const book = Object.freeze({
  name: "How JavaScript Works",
  author: {
    firstName: 'Douglas',
    lastName: 'Crockford'
  }
});
```

```
book.author.firstName = '';
```

The `book` object was changed. We can't reassign a new object to the `author`'s property, but we can modify its properties. For objects containing other objects, we should use a deepFreeze() utility function. It will freeze all the properties of all objects inside a given object.

Linting

The other option for enabling immutability is to use a linter such as ESLint. There are several plugins for it that can help us enforcing immutable objects. Such plugins are eslint-plugin-functional, eslint-plugin-fp, or eslint-plugin-immutable. We are going to use eslint-plugin-functional.

```
npm install eslint-plugin-functional --save-dev
```

After installing the plugin, change the lint config file `.eslintrc.json` to enable immutable data.

```
"plugins": [
  "functional"
],
"rules": {
  "functional/immutable-data": "error"
}
```

At this point, trying to change, delete, or add a property to an object will result in an error.

```
const counter = {
  value: 1
};
```

```
counter.value = 2;
delete counter.value;
Object.assign(counter, { value: 2 });

//Modifying properties of existing object not allowed.
```

Working with Immutable Objects

Next, let's look at how to 'change' immutable objects.

Changing an immutable object means creating a changed copied. For this is very useful to use the spread operator syntax.

Changing Properties

Here is an example of modifying an existing property:

```
const product = {
  name: 'Apple',
  quantity: 1
};

const newProduct = {
  ...product,
  quantity: 2
};
```

By using the spread syntax we first copied all the properties from the product object and then added the property that should be changed with the new value.

Adding Properties

Adding new properties can be done in a similar way. We clone the object and then add the additional properties to it.

In the next example, the product object is cloned and the type property is added.

```
const product = {
  name: 'Apple',
  quantity: 1
});
```

```
const newProduct = {
  ...product,
  type: 'fruit'
};
```

Deleting Properties

Properties can be removed using the rest operator in the destructuring syntax. In the next example, the `quantity` property is removed from the new product object by being destructured out and ignored.

```
const product = {
  name: 'Apple',
  quantity: 1
};

const {
  quantity,
  ...newProduct
} = product;

console.log(newProduct);
//{name: "Apple"}
```

From now on, in the following examples immutability is considered to be enabled using a linter tool.

Recap

An immutable object cannot be changed after creation.

We can enable immutable objects by freezing them or using a linter.

The spread operator is handy for creating changed copies of existing objects.

Chapter 03: Functions

Functions are our primary way to define and encapsulate logic.

Functions have a list of parameters and a body of statements. Depending on how the function was created, it may have a name. I will aim for having named functions most of the time.

Let's look at the main ways to define a function.

Function Declarations

A function can be created using the `function` keyword declaration, followed by the name of the function and the list of parameters. The body of the function stays inside curly braces.

```
function sum(x, y){
  return x + y;
}
```

Functions can be invoked using the function name followed by the list of arguments enclosed in parentheses.

```
sum(1,2)
//3
```

Function parameters can be initialized with default values if no value or `undefined` is passed. In the following example, if no value is given for the `step` parameter when invoking the `increment` function, it will default to 1.

```
function increment(n, step = 1){
  return n + step
}
```

```
const n = 1;
console.log(increment(n));
//2

console.log(increment(n, 2));
//3
```

Functions created this way are hoisted to the top of their scope and so they can be used before declaration. The scope of a function can be a module or an outer function in which the current function is defined.

```
sum(1,2);
//3

function sum(x, y){
   return x + y;
}
```

Functions return values. The **return** statement specifies the returned value. It also stops the execution of the function.

Function Expressions

The **function** keyword can be used to define a function inside an expression. In the function declaration, the **function** is the first keyword on the line. When that is not the case we are dealing with function expressions.

For a function expression, the name is optional, but it can be handy to have it when implementing recursive functions.

Here is a function expression.

```
const sum = function(x, y){
   return x + y;
}
```

The following is also a function expression.

```
!function start(){
   console.log('start')
}
```

Once **function** is not the first keyword on the line it becomes a function expression. The function name can be omitted and it can auto-execute.

```
!function(){
  console.log('start')
}();
//"start"
```

Arrow Function Expressions

Arrow function expressions are a compact alternative to regular function expressions.

The arrow function syntax consists of a list of parameters followed by the => symbol and then the body of the function optionally enclosed within curly braces.

```
const sum = (x, y) => x + y;

sum(1,2);
```

There is no **function** keyword this time and no **return** statement. The => symbol points to what is returned.

When the logic inside the arrow function contains multiple statements we use curly braces. This time the **return** statement is needed to return the result.

```
const sum = (x, y) => {
  return x + y;
}
```

Both function expressions are not hoisted to the top of their scope. They cannot be used before declaration.

Arity

The arity of a function describes how many parameters the function has.

- A unary function has one parameter.
- A binary function has two parameters.
- A n-ary function has n parameters.
- A nullary function has no parameters.

Pure Functions

In functional programming, functions are like mathematical functions. They do computations. These kinds of functions are called pure functions.

Pure functions calculate a new value based on the input parameters.

They are deterministic functions. That means they return the same result when called with the same input. `Math.random` and `Date.now` are not deterministic functions as they return a different result each time they are called. They cannot be used inside pure functions.

Pure functions do not modify the external environment in which the function was executed, so they do no write into the outer environment or read data that can change from the outside.

Here is an example of a pure function.

```
const number = 1.7654321;

function roundNumber(n, precision = 2){
  const noAsString = n.toFixed(precision);
  return Number.parseFloat(noAsString);
}

console.log(roundNumber(number));
//1.77
```

`roundNumber` is a pure function using other pure functions `toFixed` and `parseFloat`, to rounds a number to `n` decimals.

Changing data outside the local scope, reading data that can change from the outside, or any alteration of the external environment is a side-effect.

For the simple fact that they do only computations based on their inputs and have no side-effects they are easier to understand, test, or debug.

`Math.min`, `Math.max`, `Math.sqrt` are pure functions. In fact, all static methods from the `Math` object, with the `Math.random` exception, are pure functions.

Recap

Functions can be created using the function declarations, the function expressions, or the arrow function expressions.

In functional programming, functions should be like mathematical functions doing only computations without changing the external environment.

Chapter 04: Arrays

Arrays are indexed collections of values. Both arrays and objects are collections of values. In fact, arrays are emulated using objects.

We simply create an array using the array literal. Here is an example.

```
const arr = [1, 2, 3];
```

Detecting if a value is an array can be done with `Array.isArray`.

```
Array.isArray(arr);
//true
```

Arrays have a set of methods for data transformations.

Data transformation is one of those tasks where functional programming really shines. It makes these transformations easier to manage and understand. It does that by identifying a core set of operations all transformations do like filtering, mapping, sorting, and aggregating.

Filtering

Consider the next example selecting only the even numbers from an array.

```
const numbers = [1, 2, 3, 4];

function isEven(n) {
  return n % 2 == 0;
}

const evenNumbers = numbers.filter(isEven);
console.log(evenNumbers);
//[2, 4]
```

The `filter` method loops throw all the elements in the array and applies the `isEven` function. It creates a new array containing only those elements for which the `isEven` function returns `true`.

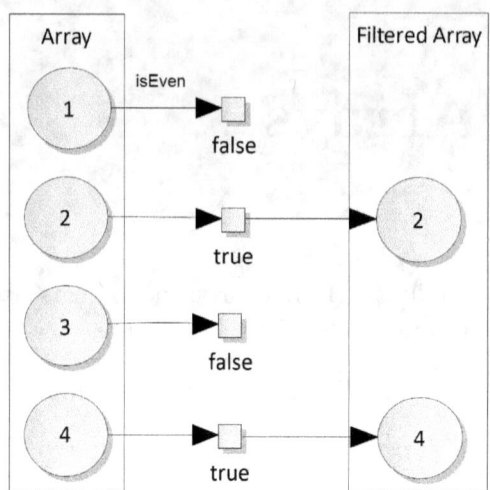

`isEven` is a predicate function.

A predicate function is a function taking an element and returning a boolean value. The predicate is a unary function.

Next, consider a list of game objects.

```
const games = [
  { title: 'Starcraft', genre: 'RTS' },
  { title: 'Command and Conquer',  genre: 'RTS' },
  { title: 'Heroes of Might and Magic', genre: 'TBS' },
  { title: 'World of Warcraft', genre : 'MMORPG'}
]
```

We are going to select only strategy games. For this, we will build a predicate function taking a game object and deciding if it is a strategy game based on its `genre` property.

```
function isStrategy(game){
  const strategyGenres = ['RTS', 'RTT', 'TBS', 'TBT'];
  return strategyGenres.includes(game.genre);
}
```

The `includes` method checks if a value is in the array and returns `true` or `false`.

Now we can use `filter` with the predicate function to select only the strategy games.

```
const strategyGames = games
  .filter(isStrategy);

console.log(strategyGames);
//[ { title: 'Starcraft', genre: 'RTS' },
//  { title: 'Command and Conquer', genre: 'RTS' },
//  { title: 'Heroes of Might and Magic', genre: 'TBS' } ]
```

Mapping

Next, we are going to apply the mapping transformation on a list of numbers.

```
const numbers = [1, 2, 3, 4];

function triple(n) {
  return n * 3;
}

const newNumbers = numbers.map(triple);
console.log(newNumbers);
//[3, 6, 9, 12]
```

The map method applies the mapping function on all elements in the array and creates a new array with the result.

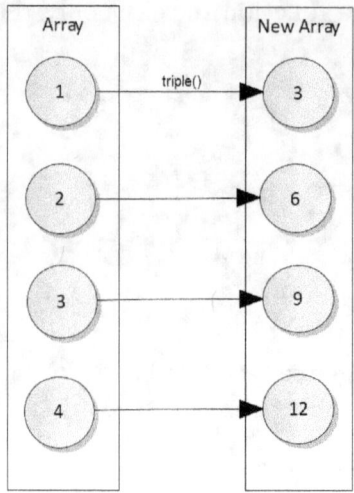

`triple` is a mapping function.

A mapping function is a function that takes an element and transforms it into a new value. It is a unary function.

Next, let's apply a mapping function on the list of game objects.

```
const games = [
  { title: 'Starcraft', genre: 'RTS' },
  { title: 'Command and Conquer',  genre: 'RTS' },
  { title: 'Heroes of Might and Magic', genre: 'TBS' },
  { title: 'World of Warcraft', genre : 'MMORPG'}
]
```

The following `toGameHtml` function takes a game object and creates the HTML string for it.

```
function toGameHtml(game){
  return `<div>${game.title}</div>`;
}
```

Template strings allow us to insert variables into strings. They are a better alternative to string concatenation. Variables inserted in template strings are surrounded by `${}`. Template strings allow the text to span multiples lines. This allows creating easier to read HTML strings.

```
function toGameHtml(game){
  return `
    <div>
```

```
    ${game.title}
  </div>`;
}
```

We can now use the mapping function to transform all game objects into HTML strings.

```
const htmlRows = games
  .map(toGameHtml);

console.log(htmlRows);
//   [ '<div>Starcraft</div>',
//     '<div>Command and Conquer</div>',
//     '<div>Heroes of Might and Magic</div>',
//     '<div>World of Warcraft</div>' ]
```

The `join` method combines all elements of an array into a new string using a separator. If no argument is provided it uses comma , as the default separator.

```
console.log(htmlRows.join(''));
//"<div>Starcraft</div>
//<div>Command and Conquer</div>
//<div>Heroes of Might and Magic</div>
//<div>World of Warcraft</div>"
```

Aggregating

Aggregation is about grouping multiple values into a single summary value.

Consider the following code.

```
const numbers = [1, 3, 5, 7];

function add(total, n) {
  return total + n;
}

const total = numbers.reduce(add, 0);
console.log(total);
//16
```

The `reduce` method reduces a list to a single value.

The **reduce** method applies the reducer function for each element in the array to compute the aggregate value. It can take a second parameter as the initial aggregate value.

add is the reducer function.

The reducer function takes the current aggregate value and the current element and returns the new aggregate value. The reducer is a binary function.

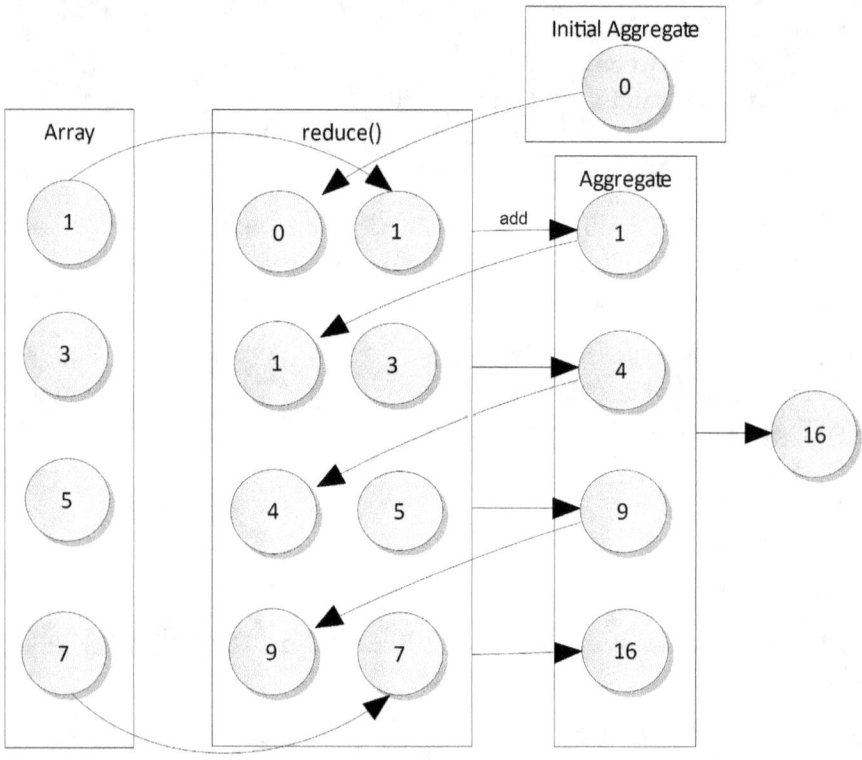

In the first iteration, the aggregate value is 0 and the current element is 1. Applying the reducer results in a new aggregate value of 1.

In the fourth iteration, the current aggregate value is 9 and the current element is 7. Applying the reducer results in the new aggregate value of 16.

Let's get back to the game objects array and compute the numbers of games for each genre.

```
const games = [
```

```
  { title: 'Starcraft', genre: 'RTS' },
  { title: 'Command and Conquer',  genre: 'RTS' },
  { title: 'Heroes of Might and Magic', genre: 'TBS' },
  { title: 'World of Warcraft', genre : 'MMORPG'}
];

function countByGenre(countMap, game){
  const count = countMap[game.genre] || 0;
  return {
    ...countMap,
    [game.genre]: count + 1
  }
}

const gamesByGenreCounts = games
.reduce(countByGenre, {});

console.log(gamesByGenreCounts);
//{ RTS: 2, TBS: 1, MMORPG: 1 }
```

`countByGenre` is the reducer function. It starts with an empty object as the aggregate value and at each step increments the number of games for the genre of the current game. Changing the `count` on the aggregate object means creating an object with the new `count`.

Sorting

The `sort` method allows sorting an array.

```
const numbers = [4, 2, 3, 1];

function asc(a, b) {
  if(a === b){
    return 0
  } else {
    if (a < b){
      return -1;
    } else {
      return 1;
    }
  }
}
```

```
const sortedNumbers = numbers.slice().sort(asc);
console.log(sortedNumbers);
//[1, 2, 3, 4]
```

The `sort` method does the sort using the compare function.

The `asc` function is the compare function. It is a binary function. It takes two values and returns -1, 0, and 1.

Consider the compare function taking two values `a` and `b`.

- It returns 0 if the values are equal
- It returns -1 if value `a` comes before value `b`
- returns 1 if value `a` comes after value `b`

`sort` is an impure method. It modifies the input array. This is why it gives a lint error. In order to do sorting, we need to clone the array first.

```
const sortedNumbers = numbers.sort(asc);
//Modifying an array is not allowed   functional/immutable-data
```

```
const sortedNumbers = numbers.slice().sort(asc);
const sortedNumbers = [...numbers].sort(asc);
```

`slice` makes a copy of the array or a copy of a part of the array. Calling `slice` with no arguments makes a copy of the array. The first parameter is the start index. The second parameter is the ending index.

Searching

`find` returns the first element that matches the predicate function. `find` returns the first match and stops. `filter` never stops and returns an array with all matches. `find` is faster than `filter`.

`findIndex` returns the index of the first match

`every` returns `true` if all elements match the predicate function. It stops at the first element that doesn't match and returns `false`.

`some` returns `true` if at least one element matches the predicate function. It stops at the first match.

All these four methods use a predicate function and stop based on the returned value.

```
const games = [
  { title: 'Starcraft 2', genre: 'RTS' },
  { title: 'Desperados 3', genre : 'RTT'},
  { title: 'Candy Crush Saga ', genre : 'Tile-matching'}
];

function isStrategy(game){
  const strategyGenres = ['RTS', 'RTT', 'TBS', 'TBT'];
  return strategyGenres.includes(game.genre);
}

const first = games.find(isStrategy);
console.log(first);
//{ title: 'Starcraft 2', genre: 'RTS' }

const firstIndex = games.findIndex(isStrategy);
console.log(firstIndex);
//0

const areAll = games.every(isStrategy);
console.log(areAll);
//false

const hasOne = games.some(isStrategy);
console.log(hasOne);
//true
```

forEach

forEach takes a function and calls it with each element in the array. It calls the function with the current element as the first argument and with the current index as the second argument.

forEach never stops and processes the whole list. It ignores the returned value.

```
const numbers = [1, 2, 3]

function log(value){
   console.log(value);
}
```

```
numbers
  .forEach(log);
//1
//2
//3
```

Impure Operations

When enabling the immutable data lint rule for objects we also force arrays to act as immutable structures.

```
"functional/immutable-data": "error"
```

It means that all the impure methods trying to modify the array like **push**, **pop**, **unshift**, or **shift** will result in lint errors.

push adds elements to the end of an array and returns the new length of the array.

pop removes and returns the last element from an array.

unshift adds elements to the beginning of an array and returns the new length of the array.

shift removes and returns the first element from an array.

```
const arr = [1, 2, 3];

arr.push(4);
arr.pop();

arr.unshift(0);
arr.shift();

//Modifying an array is not allowed
```

Changing Arrays

Next, look at how we can do the basic add, edit, and remove operations on an immutable array. Consider the array of game objects.

```
const games = [
  {id: 1, title: 'WarCraft'},
  {id: 2, title: 'X-COM: UFO Defense' }
]
```

Adding

`concat` takes one or more arrays and concatenates them together.

It can be used for adding. It creates a new array with the new value.

```
const newValue = {id: 3, title: 'The Settlers'};
const newGames = games.concat([newValue]);
console.log(newGames);

console.log(newGames);
//[ { id: 1, title: 'WarCraft' },
//  { id: 2, title: 'X-COM: UFO Defense' },
//  { id: 3, title: 'The Settlers' } ]
```

The other option for adding a value to an array is to use the spread operator. Here is an example.

```
const newGames = [...games, newValue];
```

Editing

Changing means creating a new array containing the new value at the designated index position.

We can use `map` for this. The mapping function returns the new value for the specified index otherwise it returns the existing value.

Below is an example of changing the game object at index 1.

```
const id = 1;
const newValue = { id, title: 'WarCraft 2' };

const newGames = games.map(game =>
    (game.id === id)
        ? newValue
        : game
);

console.log(newGames);
//[ { id: 1, title: 'WarCraft 2' },
//  { id: 2, title: 'X-COM: UFO Defense' } ]
```

Removing

We can remove an element from an array using `filter`. It returns a new array excluding the element at the specified index.

```
const id = 1;
const newGames = games.filter(game => game.id !== id);

console.log(newGames);
//[ { id: 2, title: 'X-COM: UFO Defense' } ]
```

Recap

`filter` selects the elements from the array that pass the predicate function.

`map` transform all elements in the array using a mapping function and creates a new array with the results.

`reduce` reduces the array to a single value using a reducer function.

`sort` sorts the elements of an array using a compare function.

Chapter 05: First-Class Functions

A language has first-class functions when it treats functions as any other values. In JavaScript, functions can be used like other values. In fact, functions are objects and thus values.

First-Class Functions

Functions can be stored in variables. We already saw such a case before.

```
const square = x => {
  return x * x;
}
```

Here, we define a function using the arrow function expression and then store the function in the **square** variable. The function infers the name of the variable. Then we can use the variable to invoke the function by adding parentheses () at the end.

```
square(3);
//9
```

Functions can be put in data structures like arrays. Look at the next example.

```
function toUpperCase(text){
  return text.toUpperCase();
}

function toLowerCase(text){
  return text.toLowerCase();
}
```

```
function trim(text){
  return text.trim();
}

const functions = [
  toUpperCase,
  toLowerCase,
  trim
];

const text = '   StARt!';
functions.forEach(f => {
  const newText = f(text);
  console.log(newText);
});
//"   START!"
//"   start!"
//"StARt!"
```

In this example, we define three functions and then put them into an array called **functions**. We then iterate through the array and call each function with a text argument. The result is displayed in the console.

When we use the function name without parentheses we refer to the function itself. When we put parentheses after the function name we refer to the result of calling the function.

Functions can be passed as arguments to other functions. In the next example, we define two functions **sum** and **multiply** and send them as an argument to another function called **doOperation**.

```
function sum(a, b){
  return a + b;
}

function multiply(a, b){
  return a * b;
}

function doOperation(operation, a, b){
  return operation(a,b)
```

```
}

doOperation(sum, 2, 3);
//5

doOperation(multiply, 2, 3);
//6
```

Functions can return other functions.

Functions can have properties and methods. For example, they have the **name** property giving access to the function name as a string.

Functions have methods like call() or apply(). These two methods basically implement the same functionality, the difference being that **call** accepts a list of arguments, while **apply** takes a single array with all arguments.

Invoking a function with arguments is also known as applying the function to those arguments. Consider the next example using the **call** method to apply the function to a set of arguments.

```
function multiply(a, b){
  return a * b;
}

multiply.call(null, 2, 3);
//6
```

Higher-Order Functions

Higher-order functions are functions that operate on other functions.

Higher-order functions take other functions as arguments, return functions, or do both.

All the array methods like **filter**, **map**, **reduce**, **sort** taking functions as inputs are higher-order functions.

The previous custom **doOperation** function is a higher-order function as it takes another function as input.

Consider the following higher-order function that returns a function.

```
const objects = [
  { id: 1 },
  { id: 2 }
];

function hasId(id){
  return function(element){
    return element.id === id;
  }
}

console.log(objects.find(hasId(1)));
//{ id: 1 }
```

`hasId` returns a function. `hasId` is a higher-order function.

Below is an example where a higher-order function creates the compare function required by the `sort` method.

```
const courses = [
  {
    title: 'Course 2',
    author: 'Author 2'
  },
  {
    title: 'Course 3',
    author: 'Author 3'
  },
  {
    title: 'Course 1',
    author: 'Author 1'
  }
];

function by(name){
  return function(a, b){
    return a[name].localeCompare(b[name]);
  }
}
```

```
courses
  .slice().sort(by('author'))
```

by is a higher-order function. It allows us to sort the list using any of the object's property that is a string.

Closures

Functions can be defined inside other functions. Besides having access to its parameters and variables, the inner function has access to parameters and variables from the outer functions.

Closure is the ability of an inner function to access variables from the outer function.

Let's start with a basic example.

```
function run(){
  const value = 1;

  function logValue(){
    console.log(value);
  }

  logValue();
}

run();
//1
```

All the variables defined inside a function are visible only inside that function. The `logValue` function is defined inside the `run` function and has access to the `value` variable.

Closures become significant when the inner functions survive the invocation of the outer function. Consider the next example.

```
function createCount(){
  let counter = 0;
  return function count(){
    counter = counter + 1;
    return counter;
  }
}
```

```
const count = createCount();

console.log(count());
//1
console.log(count());
//2
console.log(count());
//3
```

`count` has access to the `counter` variable from the outer function. `count` survives the invocation of the outer function. `count` is a closure.

Recap

Functions are values.

Functions can operate on other functions. Functions can take other functions as input or return functions.

Inner functions can access variables from the outer functions even after the outer functions have executed.

Chapter 06: Statements

An expression is a combination of one or more values, variables, operators, and functions that produce a new value. In short, an expression is a unit of code that produces a value.

A statement is an instruction to perform an action. In functional programming, everything should be an expression that produces a value. In order to achieve this, we are going to review and remove the statements that do not produce values.

Expressions

For example, `1 + 2` is an expression.

The function invocation is an expression when the function returns a value. Consider the `multiply` function.

```
function multiply(a, b){
  return a * b;
}
```

`multiply(2, 3)` is an expression.

An expression can contain other expressions. For example, the expression `multiply(2, 3+7)` contains the expression `3+7`.

The arithmetic expressions evaluate to numbers.

String expressions evaluate to strings. Here is an example:

```
"This  " + "IS A texT".toLowerCase();
//"This is a text"
```

Logical expressions evaluate to true or false. These expressions usually use logical operators like &&, ||, ! or ===.

```
1 === 2;
//false
```

An expression is a piece of code that returns a value.

Statement Declaration

There are three statements for declaring a variable `var`, `let`, and `const`.

The `var` statement declares a variable that has function scope but has no block scope. This may be confusing. The `var` declaration has become obsolete so we can disable its usage with a lint rule.

```
"no-var": "error"
```

I suggest using `const` as the default declaration and fallback to `let` as a second option. `const` declaration disables reassigning the variable and because all our values are immutable we create truly constants that cannot be reassigned or changed.

Using `const` declaration means to create a new variable each time we change something. It promotes function purity.

Conditional Statements

if Statement

The `if` statement does not necessarily return a value, so in a functional style, we should either always have the `else` branch and return a value or disable the `if` statement completely.

We are going to disable the following usage of the `if` statement.

```
const n = 3;
let isEven;

if(n % 2 === 0){
  isEven = true;
} else {
  isEven = false;
}

console.log(isEven);
```

The if statement will be allowed only if it contains an else statement and all branches have the return statement.

Here is the lint rule for this.

```
"functional/no-conditional-statement": ["error", {
  "allowReturningBranches": "ifExhaustive"
}]
```

Below is an example of the if statement with the else branch that always returns.

```
function isEven(n){
  if(n % 2 === 0){
    return true;
  } else {
    return false;
  }
}

console.log(isEven(3));
```

Conditional Operator

The better option is to use the conditional operator which is an expression that returns a value.

```
const n = 3;

const isEven = (n % 2 === 0)
  ? true
  : false

console.log(isEven);
//false
```

Below is an example of a function that returns **null** when no product object is provided, returns the **price** when it is available otherwise returns the **lastPrice**.

```
function getPrice(product){
  return product
    ? product.price
      ? product.price
```

```
            : product.lastPrice
      : null
}

console.log(getPrice(null));
//null
console.log(getPrice({lastPrice: 10}));
//10
console.log(getPrice({price:5, lastPrice: 10}));
//5
```

switch Statement

Similar to if statement, the switch statement allows writing code that does not return a value.

The following usage of the switch statement should be disabled.

```
function increment(x){
   return x + 1;
}

function decrement(x){
   return x - 1;
}

function doAction(actionName){
   switch(actionName){
     case "increment":
       number = increment(number);
     break;
     case "decrement":
       number = decrement(number);
     break;
   }
}

let number = 0;
doAction('increment')
console.log(number);
//1
```

The `switch` statement will be used only when it has a default case and all branches return a value. Check the next example.

```
function doAction(x, actionName){
  switch(actionName){
    case 'increment':
      return increment(x);
    case 'decrement':
      return decrement(x);
    default:
      return x;
  }
}

const number = 0;
const newNumber = doAction(number, 'increment');
console.log(newNumber);
//1
```

The better option is to use a map. It favors decomposing the `switch` into smaller pieces. Here is how the same logic can be re-written using an object literal as a map.

```
function increment(x){
  return x + 1;
}

function decrement(x){
  return x - 1;
}

const actionMap = {
  increment,
  decrement
}

function doAction(x, actionName){
  const action = actionMap[actionName];
  return action
    ? action(x)
    : x;
}
```

```
const number = 0;
const newNumber = doAction(number, 'increment');
console.log(number);
//1
```

Loop Statements

There are three looping statements `for`, `while` and `do-while` in the language.

for Statement

The `for` loop statement encourages mutations and side-effects. We are going to replace the `for` loops with array methods like `filter`, `map` and `reduce`. When the algorithm requires more flexibility, we can fallback to `forEach`.

The `for-in` loop iterates over the keys of an object.

```
const book = {
  title : "How JavaScript Works",
  author : "Douglas Crockford"
};

for (const propName in book) {
  console.log(book[propName])
}
```

We can implement the same logic using `Object.keys` and the array methods.

```
Object.keys(book).forEach(propName => {
  console.log(book[propName])
});
```

The `for-of` statement loops over iterable objects like arrays or strings.

```
const arr = [1, 2, 3];

for (const element of arr) {
  console.log(element);
}
```

It can be replaced with the `forEach` method.

```
arr.forEach(element => {
    console.log(element);
});
```

The `while` statement loops as long as the condition is true.

The `do-while` statement is a variant of the while loop that executes the code once, before checking the condition, then it loops as long as the condition is true.

The following lint rule disallows all loop statements, including `for`, `for-of`, `for-in`, `while`, and `do-while`.

```
"no-loop-statement": "error"
```

Disabling all loop statements is problematic. We still need at least one loop statement to rarely use for specific algorithms until the tail-call optimization is available. Here is how you can deactivate the previous loop rule on a particular line.

```
let i = 1;

// eslint-disable-next-line functional/no-loop-statement
while(i < 10){
  console.log(i);
  i = i + 1;
}
```

Disruptive Statements

There are four disruptive statements: `break`, `continue`, `throw`, and `return`. We are going to keep only the last one.

break and continue

The `break` statement "jumps out" of a loop.

The `continue` statement "jumps over" one iteration in the loop.

Both `break` and `continue` are similar to the `goto` statement and we are not going to use them. Instead, we will use array methods like `find`, `every`, or `some`.

Consider the next example breaking the loop when the searched element is found.

```
const products = [
  {id:1, name: 'apple'},
  {id:2, name:'mango'}
]

const id = 1;
let product;
for(let i=0; i<products.length; i++){
  if(products[i].id === id){
    product = products[i];
    break;
  }
}

console.log(product);
//{id:1, name: 'apple'}
```

We can implement the same logic using `find`.

```
const id = 1;
const product = products.find(p => p.id === id);
console.log(product)
```

Now, look at an example iterating over a list of words and stopping when a specific word is found.

```
const words = [
  'ability',
  'calculate',
  'calendar',
  'double',
  'door'
];

const stopTo = 'double';
for(let word of words){
  if(word === stopTo){
    break;
  }
```

```
    console.log(word);
}
```

The same logic can be implemented using `every`.

```
words.every(w => {
  if(w.startsWith(stopTo)){
    return false;
  } else {
    console.log(w);
    return true;
  }
});
```

`break` and `continue` are usually used in loops. Once we disable the loops we also disable the usage of `break` and `continue`.

`break` cannot be used in `switch` statements as they require to return on all branches.

throw

The throw statement raises an exception. Below is an example.

```
throw new Error('The errors details');
```

Exceptions are not used in functional programming, which means we need to find other alternatives for those scenarios.

For asynchronous code, the best way is to return a rejected promise when the operation fails. We will look at this scenario when discussing promises. For synchronous code, we need to return a different result when an error happens.

Here is the lint rule for disabling the `throw` statement:

```
"functional/no-throw-statement": "error"
```

Recap

Conditional statements should return a value on all branches.

The better alternative for the `if` statement is the conditional operator.

Switches can be replaced with a map.

We should use the array methods instead of the loop statements.

We are going to use only one disruptive statement **return**.

Chapter 07: Recursion

Recursion implies that a function calls itself. The recursion needs a termination. This happens when a certain condition is met and the recursive algorithm stops calling itself and returns a value.

Recursion is a method of solving a problem where the solution is found by solving smaller instances of the same problem.

Recursive Factorial

Let's start by looking at the algorithm for computing the factorial of a number in an iterative style. As you remember n! = n * (n-1)!.

```
function factorial(n) {
  let result = 1;

  let i = 2;
  while(i <= n){
    result = result * i;
    i = i + 1;
  }

  return result;
}

console.log(factorial(5));
//i=2, result=2
//i=3, result=6
//i=4, result=24
//i=5, result=120
//120
```

Here is how we can implement the same algorithm using recursion.

```
function factorial(n) {
  if (n === 0) {
    return 1;
  }
  else {
    return n * factorial(n - 1);
  }
}

//n=5 -> 5*f(4)
//n=4 -> 4*f(3)
//n=3 -> 3*f(2)
//n=2 -> 2*f(1)
//n=1 -> 1*f(0)
//n=0 -> 1 Stops!
//n=1 -> 1*f(0) = 1*1 = 1
//n=2 -> 2*f(1) = 2*1 = 2
//n=3 -> 3*f(2) = 3*2 = 6
//n=4 -> 4*f(3) = 4*6 = 24
//n=5 -> 5*f(4) = 5*24= 120

console.log(factorial(5));
//120
```

The factorial function calls itself until it has the result for n being 0. Then it resumes the execution and computes the result for n equal to 1, 2, 3, 4 and finally 5.

Below is the same recursive function refactored using the conditional operator.

```
function factorial(n) {
  return (n === 0)
    ? 1
    : n * factorial(n - 1);
}

console.log(factorial(5));
//120
```

Tail-Call Optimization

Here is another way of writing the `factorial` function.

```
function factorial(n, result = 1) {
  //console.log(`n=${n}, result=${result}`);

  return (n === 0)
    ? result
    : factorial(n - 1, n * result);
}

console.log(factorial(5));

//n=5, result=1
//n=4, result=5
//n=3, result=20
//n=2, result=60
//n=1, result=120
//n=0, result=120
//120
```

Notice that this time, once the function arrives at the stopping condition it returns the result. It does not need to go back and resume the previous calls to return the end result. It returns when the ending condition is met because it has all the necessary data.

A recursive function is tail-recursive when the recursive call is the last thing the function does.

The tail-recursive functions should be optimized by the compiler and should perform better.

At the moment of writing the tail-call optimization is not implemented by the major browsers.

Stack Overflow Error

Consider the following function that computes the sum of all values from 0 to 10000 in an iterative style

```
function sumAll(n) {
  let total = 0;
  let i = 1;
```

```
  while(i <= n){
    total = total + i;
    i = i + 1;
  }

  return total;
}
```

```
console.log(sumAll(10000));
//50005000
```

Below is the equivalent code written with the tail-call optimization.

```
function sumAll(n, i = 0, result = 0) {
  return (i > n)
    ? result
    : sumAll(n, i + 1, i + result);
}
```

```
console.log(sumAll(5));
//15
```

Calling the recursive function with a larger number leads to the stack overflow error.

```
console.log(sumAll(10000));
//Maximum call stack size exceeded
```

Recursion can lead to the "Maximum call stack size exceeded" error message.

JavaScript reserves for each function call a call-stack, a fixed amount of memory to keep information about the call. Information is added to the call-stack like in any other stack last-in, first-out. Each recursive call adds a new stack-frame to the call-stack. If the recursive calls create too many stack-frames the stack overflow error is thrown.

The tail-recursive functions should not create a new stack frame for each function call, but rather use a single stack frame.

In theory, any loop can be implemented with recursion. Because of the missing implementation of the tail-call optimization, it is not practical to replace any kind of loop with recursion. At the time of writing, the tail-call recursive implementation of a loop may have a performance penalty or may lead to stack-overflow error.

Trampoline

Trampolining is a technique that allows us to work with tail-recursive functions in a language that does not have the tail-call optimization.

First, it requires to rewrite the original tail-call function to return thunks instead of returning the actual values. In our example, it means that instead of returning the result of `sumAll(n, i + 1, i + result)` we return a nullary function returning that result.

```
function sumAll(n, i = 0, result = 0) {
  return (i > n)
      ? () => result
      : () => sumAll(n, i + 1, i + result);
}
```

A thunk is a function taking no arguments that invokes another function with all the necessary arguments and returns the result.

For example, the following function is a thunk.

```
const sum100Thunk = () => sumAll(100);
```

The `sum100Thunk` function takes no arguments and returns the result of invoking `sumAll` with the specific arguments.

After converting the original function to return thunks we need the `trampoline` utility function that loops in an iterative way and invokes the thunk functions. The loop continues as long as the thunks return other thunk functions.

```
function trampoline(f) {
  return function(...args){
    let result = f(...args);
    while (typeof(result) === 'function'){
      result = result();
    }

    return result;
  }
}
```

```
const _sumAll = trampoline(sumAll);

console.log(_sumAll(10000));
//50005000
```

Trampolining is a solution to a problem we should not have and also comes with its own overhead. It basically allows us to convert the recursive function to an iterative loop.

Traversing a Tree

Recursion can be used to implement specific algorithms that are easier to solve this way.

In the next example, recursion is used to traverse a tree and create an array with the top selected node values.

We start by defining the tree, beginning with the root node object containing other node objects. Each node has the **value** and **checked** properties.

```
const tree = {
  value: 0,
  checked: false,
  children: [{
    value: 1,
    checked: true,
    children: [{
      value: 11,
      checked: true,
      children: null
    }]
  }, {
    value: 2,
    checked: false,
    children: [{
      value: 22,
      checked: true,
      children: null
    },{
      value: 23,
      checked: true,
      children: null
    }]
```

```
    }]
}
```

Here is a visual representation of this tree.

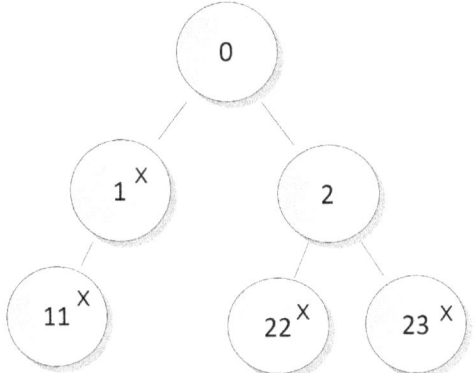

We want to get the values of the top selected nodes. That means we don't need all the checked values from the tree. If the parent node is checked we don't have to take the checked values from its children.

```
function toChildTopSelection(selection, childNode){
   return selection.concat(getTopSelection(childNode));
}

function getTopSelection(node){
   return node.checked
      ?   [node.value]
      :   node.children !== null
          ? node.children.reduce(toChildTopSelection, [])
          : []
}

getTopSelection(tree);
//[1, 22, 23]
```

`getTopSelection` takes a tree object and returns an array with the top selected values. If the node is checked it returns the value of that node as an array with a single element. When the node is not checked and has child nodes it returns the top selection of those child nodes. `getTopSelection` is called for each child node inside the tree until the recursive calls stop at the nodes being checked. Finding a node that is checked is the ending condition. `getTopSelection` is not called for the child nodes of a node that is checked.

Recap

A recursive function is a function that calls itself until a condition is met.

Recursion offers a simpler solution to a set of problems like traversing trees.

Any iterative loop can be implemented with recursion but this is not practical until the tail-call optimization is supported by major browsers.

Chapter 08: Pipelines and Currying

Pipelines are the typical use case for functional programming.

Currying is commonly used when creating pipelines because the functions defining the flow of transformations expect one argument.

Pipelines

A pipeline is a series of data transformations where the output of one transformation is the input of the next one.

Pipelines enable us to write data transformations in a more expressive way. Consider the next code:

```
function capitalize(text) {
  return text.charAt(0).toUpperCase() + text.slice(1);
}

function shortenText(text) {
  return text.substring(0, 8).trim();
}

const shortText =
  shortenText(capitalize("this is a long text"));
console.log(shortText);
//"This is"
```

We can write these transformations in a more expressive way using the `pipe` utility from a functional library like lodash or ramda.

```
npm i lodash --save
```

Here is how the transformations look like in a pipeline.

```
import { pipe } from 'lodash/fp';

const shortText = pipe(
  capitalize,
  shortenText
)("this is a long text");

console.log(shortText);
//"This is"
```

The initial text is the input in the pipeline. `capitalize` is the first function to process the text. Then the output of this transformation goes as input to the next one `shortenText`. Then the pipeline finishes and we get the result.

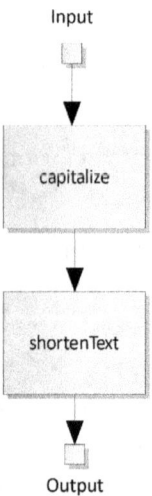

Chaining

Chaining is a more common form of defining a pipeline. It requires to work with an object.

Consider the following list of debts.

```
const debts = [
  {
    contractNo : 1,
    daysSinceLastPayment: 91,
```

```
    currency : 'EUR'
  },
  {
    contractNo : 2,
    daysSinceLastPayment: 35,
    currency : 'USD'
  },
  {
    contractNo : 3,
    daysSinceLastPayment: 45,
    currency : 'USD'
  }
];
```

Here is how we can define a pipeline of transformations using chaining.

```
const newDebts = debts
  .filter(isEur)
  .map(toDebtView);

function isEur(debt){
  return debt.currency === "EUR";
}

function toDebtView(debt){
  return {
    ...debt,
    priority : getPriority(debt)
  }
}

function getPriority(debt){
  const days = debt.daysSinceLastPayment;
  return days > 90
    ? 1
    : days > 60
      ? 2
      : 3;
}
```

First, the debt list is filtered using `isEur` predicate function. Then the result of this operation is transformed using the `toDebtView` mapping function.

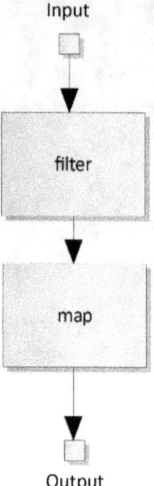

The Identity Function

The identity function is a unary function that returns the value it gets as its argument.

In mathematics, it is defined as `f(x) = x`.

```
function identity(value){
   return value;
}
```

If we put this transformation in the previous pipeline it will just create a copy of the array.

The `logIdentity` function gives a way to inspect the data in the pipeline without affecting the flow. It returns the argument it gets but also logs it to the console.

```
function logIdentity(value){
   console.log(value);
   return value;
}

debts
   .filter(isEur)
   .map(logIdentity)
```

```
.map(toDebtView)
.map(logIdentity);
```

Currying

Currying is a technique for changing a function expecting **n** arguments into a series of **n** functions each expecting one argument.

Consider the case of filtering a list of words.

```
const words = [
  'ability',
  'calculate',
  'calendar',
  'double',
  'door'
];

function startsWith(word, term){
  return word.startsWith(term);
}

words
  .filter(w => startsWith(w, 'a'))
  .forEach(console.log);
```

Now, look at the same code refactored using currying.

```
function startsWith(term){
  return function(word){
    return word.startsWith(term);
  }
}

words
  .filter(startsWith('a'))
  .forEach(console.log);
```

`startsWith` is a curried function. Instead of taking two parameters, it takes only one and returns a function accepting the second parameter. Notice also that the curried version has the parameters in the reverse order compared to the initial version taking two parameters.

You may find it clearer when the curried version is written using the arrow syntax.

```
const startsWith = term => word => {
  return word.startsWith(term);
}
```

Another option is to create the curried version of a function using an auto-curry utility function. Here is an example using the `curry` utility from lodash.

```
import { curry } from 'lodash/fp';

const startsWith = curry(function(term, word) {
    return word.startsWith(term);
});
```

Reduce Pipeline

The `reduce` method uses also a pipeline. Let's look again at the code and analyze the data flow.

```
const numbers = [1, 3, 5];

function add(total, n) {
    return total + n;
}

const total = numbers.reduce(add, 0);
console.log(total);
//9
```

At each step, the reducer takes as input the result of the previous reducer call as the aggregation value. Here is the pipeline.

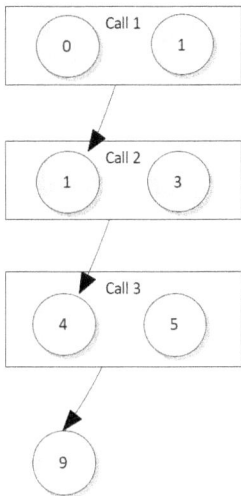

The aggregation value at the first step is 0. After invoking the reducer the output of this transformation 1 goes as input to the next reducer call. Again after invoking the reducer, the output 4 goes as input to the next reducer call and so on.

reduce creates a pipeline where at each step we get as input the result of the previous reducer call and the current element.

Recap

A pipeline defines a series of data transformations where the output of one transformation function is the input for the next one.

Currying is a technique for breaking down a function that takes multiple arguments into a series of functions each taking only one argument.

Chapter 09: Functors

Next, we are going to explore functors.

Let's start with a set of data transformations. Consider the next example:

```
function toCelsius(kelvin){
  const celsius = (kelvin - 273.15);
  return Math.round(celsius * 100) / 100;
}

function describeTemperature(temperature){
  return temperature < 0
    ? "Freezing"
    : temperature < 15
      ? "Cold"
      : temperature < 28
        ? "Warm"
        : "Hot";
}

const kelvin = 300;
const celsius = toCelsius(kelvin);
const description = describeTemperature(celsius);

console.log(celsius);
//26.85
console.log(description)
//"Warm"
```

As you can see, the point of this piece of code is to apply two changes to a single value. It starts with the Kelvin temperature and applies the `toCelsius` transformation, then on the result, it applies the `describeTemperature` function.

It will be nicer to be able to chain these transformations on the initial value and create a pipeline. Here is how it may look like:

```
Mappable(300)
  .map(toCelsius)
  .map(describeTemperature)
```

This is the kind of situation where functors are helpful.

Functors

A functor is an object with a map operation that satisfies the functor laws.

We can simply create a functor as an object with a `map` method. Consider the following function:

```
function F(value){

  function map(f){
    const newValue = f(value);
    return F(newValue);
  }

  return {
    map
  }
}
```

F creates an object with the `map` method wrapping a `value`. `map` takes a transformation function, applies it to the wrapped value, and returns a new object wrapping the new value.

F is called a factory function. F returns an object containing a closure, `map`, accessing the `value` variable from its parent.

The F factory function creates a functor.

Functor Laws

Functors must respect identity and composition laws.

Identity Law

Passing the identity function into the `map` operation of a functor should result in the same functor, meaning a functor storing the same value.

Consider the `identity` function.

```
function identity(n){
   return n;
}
```

`functor.map(identiy) === functor`

Let's verify the identity law on our functor.

`const functor = F(1);`

```
const newFunctor = functor.map(identity);
//F(1)
```

Composition Law

Function composition is an operation that takes two functions `f` and `g` and produces a new function `h` where `h(x) = g(f(x))`. In this operation, the function `g` is applied to the result of applying the function `f` to `x`.

We can say that function composition is the operation of applying a function to the result of another function.

Functors must respect the composition law, meaning that:

`functor.map(f).map(g) === functor.map(x => g(f(x)))`

Let's verify the composition law.

```
function increment(n){
   return n + 1;
}

function double(n){
   return n * 2;
}

F(1)
  .map(increment)
  .map(double)
```

```
//F(4)

F(1)
  .map(n => double(increment(n)))
  //F(4)
```

Category Theory

A category is a collection of values that are linked by arrows.

A category has two main properties, the ability to compose the arrows associatively, and the existence of an identity arrow for each value.

The arrows, also known as morphisms, are functions mapping between the values in the category.

Here is a representation of a category with three values.

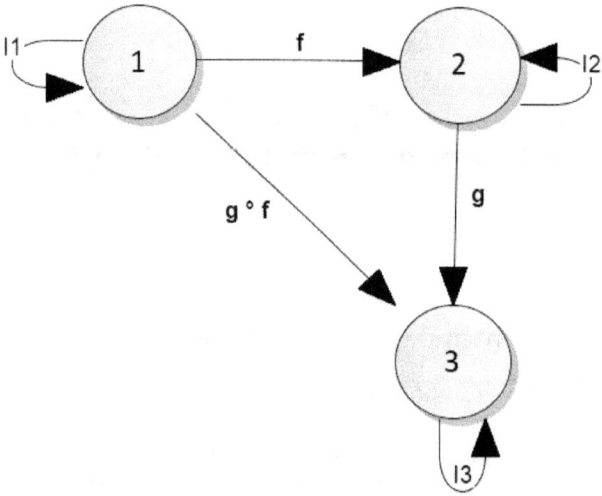

The category in this example has three values: 1, 2, 3, and three functions mapping between these values. The f function maps 1 to 2. The g function maps 2 to 3. The function h mapping from 1 to 3 is equal to g(f(1)). For each value applying the identity function results in the same value.

Functors in Practice

In practice, functors are helpful at chaining operations.

What is important for us from the development perspective is to know when something is a functor. If it is, we can inspect its value with the identity function and we use function composition.

The functor we have created is called the identity functor.

Take into consideration our initial set of data transformations. Here is how we can chain the two transformations on a value using the identity functor.

```
F(300)
  .map(toCelsius)
  .map(describeTemperature)
```

We can inspect the value inside using the impure variation of the identity function that logs the value in the console.

```
function logIdentity(value){
  console.log(value);
  return value;
}

F(300)
  .map(toCelsius)
  .map(logIdentity) //26.85
  .map(describeTemperature)
  .map(logIdentity) //"Warm"
```

We get the same result also when applying function composition.

```
F(300)
  .map(x => describeTemperature(toCelsius(x)))
  .map(logIdentity)
  //"Warm"
```

Below is an example of applying function composition using the `compose` utility from a functional library like lodash.

```
import { compose } from 'lodash/fp'

F(300)
  .map(compose(describeTemperature, toCelsius))
  .map(logIdentity)
  //"Warm"
```

Arrays

Arrays are mappable. The `map` method iterates over the collection and applies the `map` function to each value in the array.

Let's verify the functor laws on the array.

Applying the identity function on an array creates a copy of it.

```
[1, 2, 3]
  .map(identity)
  .map(logIdentity);
//1
//2
//3
```

Next, check the composition law.

```
[1, 2, 3]
  .map(increment)
  .map(double)
  .map(logIdentity);
//4
//6
//8

[1, 2, 3]
  .map(x => double(increment(x)))
  .map(logIdentity);
//4
//6
//8
```

The built-in arrays have a `map` operation that satisfies the functor laws. The built-in arrays are functors.

A simple functor wrapping a single value can be created on the fly using an array with a one value

```
[300]
  .map(toCelsius)
  .map(describeTemperature)
  .map(logIdentity);
//"Warm"
```

```
[300]
  .map(x => describeTemperature(toCelsius(x)))
  .map(logIdentity);
//"Warm"
```

An array wrapping a single value basically emulates the identity functor.

Recap

A category is a collection of values, with arrows between these values. Arrows represent mapping functions. Applying the identity function on any value returns that value.

Functors are mappable objects that respect identity and composition.

Functors offer us a helpful way of creating pipelines of data transformations over the wrapped value.

Chapter 10: Monads

A functor is an object that wraps a value and enables mapping. The mapping operation satisfies the functor laws.

A monad is an object that wraps a value and enables mapping and flat mapping. The flat mapping operation satisfies the monad laws.

Flat Mapping

Let's look again at the `map` method available on the array functor. Applying a mapping function that returns a value results in a new array wrapping the transformed values.

```
function toUpperCase(text){
  return text.toUpperCase();
}

const arr = ["raspberry strawberry", "blueberry"]
  .map(toUpperCase);

console.log(arr);
//[ 'RASPBERRY STRAWBERRY', 'BLUEBERRY' ]
```

The initial array has two text values. After applying the transformation we get an array containing two text values with uppercase letters.

Check what happens when we apply a mapping function that returns an array.

```
function split(text){
  return text.split(' ');
}
```

```
const arr = ["raspberry strawberry", "blueberry"]
  .map(split)

console.log(arr);
//[ [ 'raspberry', 'strawberry' ], [ 'blueberry' ] ]
```

The `split` function splits a string into an array of substrings using a separator. Each substring represents a word in the original text.

Applying the `split` mapping function results in an array containing two other arrays. Each sub-array is a collection of strings.

Flat mapping is similar to mapping, but it unwraps the return type.

Next, take a look at applying the same mapping function using the `flatMap` method available on arrays.

```
const arr = ["raspberry strawberry", "blueberry"]
  .flatMap(split)

console.log(arr);
//[ 'raspberry', 'strawberry', 'blueberry' ]
```

The `flatMap` method first maps each element in the arrays using the mapping function, then flattens the result into a new array. The same outcome can be achieved by first using `map` and then flatten the result using `flat` with depth 1.

```
const arr = ["raspberry strawberry", "blueberry"]
  .map(split)
  .flat();

console.log(arr);
//[ 'raspberry', 'strawberry', 'blueberry' ]
```

`flat` creates a new array with all sub-array values concatenated into it. It uses recursion to concatenate values up to the specified depth.

```
const arr = [1, [2, 3]];

console.log(arr.flat());
//[ 1, 2, 3 ]
```

Monads

We can simply create a monad as an object with the `map` and `flatMap` methods. Consider the following `M` function:

```
function M(value){

  function map(f){
    const newValue = f(value);
    return M(newValue);
  }

  function flatMap(f){
    const newValue = f(value);
    return newValue;
  }

  return {
    map,
    flatMap
  }
}
```

`M` is a factory function that creates an object wrapping a value and having two methods to modify it, `map` and `flatMap`.

`map` takes a transformation function and uses it to create a new value then uses the `M` factory function to create an object wrapping that new value.

`flatMap` uses the transformation function to compute a new value and returns it.

`M` is the monad constructor. It takes a value and returns a monad wrapping the value.

`M` is called the identity monad.

Monad Laws

There are three laws monads should respect.

Left Identity

Consider `f` as a mapping function returning a monad. Passing the `f` function into the `flatMap` operation of a monad wrapping the value `x` should result in the same monad as invoking the function `f(x)`.

```
M(x).flatMap(f) === f(x)
```

Let's verify the left identity law on our monad.

```
function f(){
  return M(2)
}

M(1)
  .flatMap(f);
  //M(2)

f(1);
  //M(2)
```

Right Identity

Passing the M function into the `flatMap` operation of a monad wrapping a value should result in monad wrapping the same value.

```
monad.flatMap(M) === monad
```

Check the law using the M custom monad.

```
M(1)
  .flatMap(M)
  //M(1)
```

Associativity

Monads must respect the associativity law, meaning that:

```
monad.flatMap(f).flatMap(g)
  === monad.flatMap(x => f(x).flatMap(g))
```

Let's test the law.

```
function f(){
  return M(2)
}
```

```
function g(){
  return M(3)
}

M(1)
  .flatMap(f)
  .flatMap(g);
  //M(3)

M(1)
  .flatMap(n => f(n).flatMap(g));
  //M(3)
```

Alternative Creation and Naming

The flat mapping method comes with different names like bind, chain, or just flatMap. There is also the practice to create the monad with a different method called unit. unit does the same thing as the M factory function does, it creates a new monad.

Below is an example of defining a monad using this alternative naming.

```
export default (function defineMonad(){
  function M(value){
    function map(f){
      const newValue = f(value);
      return M(newValue);
    }

    function bind(f){
      const newValue = f(value);
      return newValue;
    }

    return {
      map,
      bind
    }
  }

  function unit(value){
```

```
    return M(value);
  }

  return {
    unit
  }
})();
```

unit creates a new monad wrapping a value.

bind defines the flat map operation.

Here is how the monad can be created and used.

```
import M from './M';

function f(){
  return M.unit(2)
}

M.unit(1).bind(f)
//M 2
```

Below you can review how the monad rules can be written in this case.

Left identity

```
M.unit(1).bind(f)
//M 2
```

Right identity

```
M.unit(1).bind(M.unit)
//M 1
```

Associativity

```
M.unit(1).bind(f).bind(g)
//M 3

M.unit(1).bind(x => f(x).bind(g))
//M 3
```

You may also find bind described as a separate function and not as a method on the monad object: bind(monad, f). This translates to monad.bind(f) when bind is a method on the monad object.

It is more helpful to describe `bind` as a method.

Let's take a look at how we can translate the monad laws from the function form to the method form.

The following three ways of describing the monad laws are equivalent.

Left identity

```
bind(unit(x), f) === f(x)

M.unit(x).bind(f) === f(x)

M(x).flatMap(f) === f(x)
```

Note that in the last line, `M` is used as the constructor function. `M(x)` is equivalent to `M.unit(x)` and is also equivalent to `unit(x)`.

Right identity

```
bind(monad, unit)   === monad
monad.bind(M.unit)  === monad
monad.flatMap(M)    === monad
```

Associativity

```
bind(bind(monad, f), g)
  === bind(monad, x => bind(f(x), g))

monad.bind(f).bind(g)
  === monad.bind(x => f(x).bind(g))

monad.flatMap(f).flatMap(g)
  === monad.flatMap(x => f(x).flatMap(g))
```

This being said, I consider that the first implementation of the identity monad as an object with `map` and `flatMap` method is easier to work with.

Arrays

Arrays have both the `map` and `flatMap` methods. Let's check the monad laws on them.

First, we need a constructor function that can create the array from a value.

```
function M(value){
  return [value];
}
```

We don't need to define such a function because there is already one that does that. It is called `Array.of()`.

```
M('apple')
//['apple']

Array.of('apple')
//['apple']
```

As you noticed, when creating an array with `Array.of`, $M(x)$ translates to `Array.of(x)`.

Consider the following two functions taking a value and returning an array.

```
//f
function duplicate(word){
  return [word, word]
}

//g
function split(text){
  return text.split(" ");
}
```

Next check the three laws.

Left identity

```
//M(x).flatMap(f) === f(x)

Array.of('mango')
  .flatMap(duplicate)
  //['mango', 'mango']

duplicate('mango');
//['mango', 'mango']
```

Right identity

```
//monad.flatMap(M) === monad
```

```
Array.of('lemon')
  .flatMap(Array.of)
//['lemon']

Array.of('lemon')
//['lemon']
```

Associativity

```
//monad.flatMap(f).flatMap(g)
//   === monad.flatMap(x => f(x).flatMap(g)))

Array.of('orange kiwi')
  .flatMap(split)
  .flatMap(duplicate);
//[ 'orange', 'orange', 'kiwi', 'kiwi' ]

Array.of('orange kiwi')
  .flatMap(s => split(s).flatMap(duplicate))
//[ 'orange', 'orange', 'kiwi', 'kiwi' ]
```

The built-in array has all the things a monad needs. It has the `map` and `flatMap` operations and they obey the laws. The built-in arrays are monads.

Recap

A functor is an object with a `map` operation that obeys certain laws.

A monad is an object with `map` and `flatMap` operations that obey certain laws.

Functors apply a function to a wrapped value.

Monads apply a function that returns a wrapped value to a wrapped value.

In essence, a monad is simply a wrapper around a value. We can create it with an object that stores a single value and offers support for mapping and flat mapping. In the next chapters, we are going to explore a few practical monads.

Chapter 11: Immutable Collections

A collection is anything that can be iterated over.

Immutable collections return a new collection on "change" operations. We are going to look at such collections available in the Immutable.JS library. Install it first.

```
npm install immutable --save
```

List

Lists are indexed collections, similar to arrays. In fact, they can be created from arrays.

```
import { List } from 'immutable';

const emptyList = List();
// List []

const list = List([
    { name: 'Rhodes' },
    { name: 'Malaga' }
]);
// List [
//   { name: 'Rhodes' },
//   { name: 'Malaga' }]
```

List() creates a new immutable List containing the values provided as the argument. `List` is a factory function and does not use the `new` keyword.

Editing an element

set(index, value) allows us to edit an element at a specific index in the collection. It returns a new List containing the modification. The element at the specified index position will be replaced.

```
const newList = list.set(0, { name: 'Riomaggiore' });
// List [
//   { name: 'Riomaggiore' },
//   { name: 'Malaga' }]

console.log(list === newList);
//false
```

Adding an element

push(...values) returns a new List with the provided **values** appended. It can be used to add a new value to the list. Below is an example.

```
const newList = list.push({name: 'Funchal'});
// List [
//   { name: 'Rhodes' },
//   { name: 'Malaga' },
//   { name: 'Funchal'}]
```

Adding can also be done with concat(...values). It concatenates a new collection to the existing one. To add a single value we call it with an array containing one value.

```
const newList = list.concat([{name: 'Funchal'}]);
// List [
//   { name: 'Rhodes' },
//   { name: 'Malaga' },
//   { name: 'Funchal'}]
```

unshift(...values) returns a new List with the provided **values** prepended.

Deleting an element

delete(index) deletes the element at the specified index and returns a new List containing the modification.

```
const newList = list.delete(0);
// List [{ name: 'Malaga' }]
```

`delete` has the `remove` alias.

pop() returns a new List with the last element removed.

shift() returns a new List with the first element removed.

Clearing the list

clear() returns a new List with no values.

```
const newList = list.clear();

console.log(newList)
// List []
```

Data Transformation

We can work with lists similar to arrays. Lists have the `filter`, `map`, `flatMap`, `reduce`, and `sort` methods working like in arrays. The `sort` method this time is a pure method returning a new collection.

Here is an example of using the `filter` method to select only the destinations to a specific country from a list of destination objects.

```
import { List } from 'immutable';

const list = List([
  { name: 'Cascais', country: 'Portugal'},
  { name: 'Sintra', country: 'Portugal' },
  { name: 'Nerja', country: 'Spain' },
]);

function inCountry(country){
  return function(destination){
    return destination.country === country;
  }
}

list
  .filter(inCountry('Portugal'))
//List [
// {name:'Cascais',country:'Portugal'},
// {name:'Sintra',country:'Portugal'}]
```

Note that `inCountry` is a curried function.

Lists are monads as they support both mapping and flat mapping. We can check the functor and monad laws on them, in a similar way we did for the built-in arrays, and find they are being respected.

Finding Elements

Lists have methods for retrieving data.

get(index) returns the element associated with the provided index.

first() returns the first element in the collection. In case the collection is empty, it returns `undefined`. In a similar way, last() returns the last element in the collection.

find() returns the first element for which the predicate function returns `true`. findLast() returns the last element for which the predicate function returns `true`. Below is an example of using these two methods on the previous list.

```
import { List } from 'immutable';

const list = List([
    { name: 'Cascais', country: 'Portugal'},
    { name: 'Sintra ', country: 'Portugal' },
    { name: 'Nerja ', country: 'Spain' },
]);

const destination = list.find(inCountry('Portugal'));
//{ name: 'Cascais', country: 'Portugal' }

const otherDestionation = list.findLast(inCountry('Portugal'));
//{ name: 'Sintra ', country: 'Portugal' }
```

Map

A map is a collection of key-value pairs. Immutable maps accept keys of any type.

Here is an example of creating a map of country objects by id.

```
import { Map } from 'immutable';
```

```
const countryMap = Map({
  "1": { name: 'Italy'},
  "2": { name: 'Portugal'},
  "3": { name: 'UK'}
});
```

get(key) returns the value associated with the given key.

```
console.log(countryMap.get("3"));
//{ name: 'UK' }
```

set(key, value) returns a new Map containing the key-value pair. If the key already exists, its value is replaced. If the key does not exist, it will be added. set can be used for adding and editing a key-value pair.

```
const newMap = countryMap.set("2", { name: 'Spain'});
console.log(newMap.get("2"));
//{ name: 'Spain' }
```

has(key) returns true if the given key exists within the map, otherwise, it returns false.

delete(key) returns a new Map with the specified key removed.

```
const newMap = countryMap.delete("3");

console.log(newMap.has("3"));
//false

console.log(newMap.get("3"));
//undefined
```

clear() returns a new Map containing no key-values pairs.

Data Transformation

Maps support both the `filter` and `map` operations.

map(mapper) returns a new Map on which the `mapper` function was applied to all values.

filter(predicate) returns a new Map containing only the key-value pairs for which the `predicate` function returns true. The predicate function is applied to the value.

Recap

Both `List` and `Map` offer a nicer public interface for working with immutable collections.

Lists have the `filter`, `map`, `reduce`, and `sort` methods working similar to the ones available in arrays.

These immutable data structures are highly optimized. Lists have efficient addition and removal from both the end and the beginning of the list of O(1) complexity.

Chapter 12: Lazy Transformations

Array operations like `filter`, `map`, `reduce` make transformations a lot easier to read and understand, but as you noticed these transformations create a new array at each step. This may create performance penalties for large arrays of thousands of records.

Next, we are going to explore solutions to these cases.

Transducers

The fact is that all transformations can be expressed using the reducer function. We can do filtering using the reducer function, mapping can be done using the reducer function, and so on.

Here is an implementation of the mapping transformation using `reduce`.

```
function map(transform) {
  return function reducer(arr, value) {
    const newValue = transform(value);
    return [...arr, newValue];
  }
}

function double(n){
  return n * 2;
}

const numbers = [1, 2, 3];
const newNumbers = numbers.reduce(map(double), []);
//[2, 4, 6]
```

Below is the filtering transformation implemented using **reduce**.

```
function filter(test) {
  return function reducer(arr, value) {
    if (test(value)) {
      return [...arr, value]
    } else {
      return arr;
    }
  }
}

function isEven(n){
  return n % 2 === 0;
}

const numbers = [1, 2, 3, 4];
const newNumbers = numbers.reduce(filter(isEven), []);
//[2, 4]
```

Note that **reduce** does not stop and processes all the values in the array. The **find** method stops when it finds the value. The equivalent implementation of **find** using the reduce method performs worse because it loops through all the elements.

```
function find(test) {
  return function reducer(foundValue, value) {
    if (test(value) && !foundValue) {
      return value
    } else {
      return foundValue;
    }
  }
}

function isEven(n){
  return n % 2 === 0;
}

const numbers = [1, 2, 3, 4];
const element = numbers.reduce(find(isEven), undefined);
//2
```

Knowing all these, when doing transformations instead of building a new array at each step we can build a new reducer function.

Consider the next example creating an array at each step.

```
function isEven(n){
  return n % 2 === 0;
}

function double(n){
  return n * 2;
}

const numbers = [1, 2, 3, 4];
const newNumbers =
  numbers
    .filter(isEven) //[2, 4]
    .map(double); //[4, 8]
```

The first `filter` created an intermediate array [2, 4] that is then used by the `map` method.

Let's see what it means to arrive at the same result by building a reducer that does all the transformations instead of building intermediate arrays.

This means that `filter` creates a new reducer applying filtering, and `map` takes this reducer and creates a new one applying the mapping transformation.

Here is the implementation of a filter function that takes a reducer and creates a new one that applies the predicate test.

```
function filter(test) {
  return function(reducer){
    return function filterReducer(arr, value){
      if(test(value)){
        return reducer(arr, value);
      } else {
        return arr;
      }
    }
  }
}
```

It may look better if we use the arrow function and the conditional operator to defined this curried function.

```
const filter = test => reducer => {
  return function filterReducer(arr, value){
    return test(value)
      ? reducer(arr, value)
      : arr
  }
}
```

Here is the map function taking a reducer and returning a new reducer that applies the mapping transformation to all values.

```
const map = transform => reducer => {
  return function mapReducer(arr, value){
    const newValue = transform(value);
    return reducer(arr, newValue);
  }
}
```

All these functions work on reducers, so we need an initial reducer to work on. This will be a function that just makes a copy of the existing array.

```
const toArrayReducer = (arr, value) => {
  return [...arr, value]
};
```

Let's use these functions to refactor the previous transformations.

```
function isEven(n){}
function double(n){}

const numbers = [1, 2, 3, 4];
const filterTransducer = filter(isEven);
const mapTransducer = map(double);

const newNumbers = numbers
  .reduce(
    filterTransducer(
      mapTransducer(toArrayReducer)
    ),
    []);
//[4, 8]
```

The functions created by `filter` and `map` are called transducers.

A transducer takes a reducer and returns a new reducer. In other words, a transducer is a function that takes a reducer function as input and returns a new reducer function. A transducer is a higher-order function.

The transformation may look better if we use the `compose` utility. Below is an example where the filter and map transducers are applied to the `toArrayReducer` reducer. We end up with one reducer doing all the necessary transformations.

```
import { compose } from 'lodash/fp';

const newReducer = compose(
  filter(isEven),
  map(double)
)(toArrayReducer);
```

We can then apply this reducer to the original array.

```
const newNumbers = numbers.reduce(newReducer, []));
```

Transducers come with their overhead. They need to iterate through all the items at each transformation because the `reduce` method does not stop. They need to work on a primary reducer, so an initial transformation that was not required before is needed now. Nevertheless, they give us an insight on how to chain transformations without creating additional collections.

Sequence

Lazy sequences allow us to efficiently chain transformation methods like `map` and `filter` without creating intermediate collections. We are going to look at the lazy sequence provided by Immutable.js called `Seq`.

The `Seq` collection is immutable. Once created, it cannot be modified. Any "change" operation returns a new `Seq`.

Here is an example where an array is converted to a sequence and then transform without creating other intermediate arrays.

```
import { Seq } from 'immutable';

function isEven(n){
    return n % 2 === 0;
```

```
}

function double(n){
    return n * 2;
}

const sequence = Seq([ 1, 2, 3, 4])
  .filter(isEven)
  .map(double);
```

Then we can convert back to an array data structure using the toArray() method.

```
const newArray = sequence.toArray();
//[4, 8]
```

Note that these conversions to the native array using **toArray** can be slow so once we created a sequence and made the transformations we should stick with it and use it.

Range

Range returns a sequence of numbers from **start** to the **end**. When called with no arguments it starts from 0. When no **end** argument is provided it creates an infinite sequence. It also accepts a third argument, a **step**, defining the increment.

Range is a lazy sequence that generates integer numbers in order. Here is an example of a Range generating the numbers 1, 2, 3.

```
import { Range } from 'immutable';

function logIdentity(n){
  console.log(n);
  return n;
}

Range(1, 4)
     .forEach(logIdentity);
//1
//2
//3
```

Now, look at an example of generating prime numbers. Check how we can refactor the `for` loop out using the `Range` sequence.

```
for(let i=0; i<10; i++){
  if(isPrime(i)){
    console.log(i)
  }
}
//2
//3
//5
//7

function isPrime(number){
  if (number <= 1){
    return false;
  }

  for (let i=2; i<=number/2; i++){
    if (number % i === 0 ){
      return false;
    }
  }

  return true;
}
```

We can start by replacing the first loop printing the numbers to the console.

```
import { Range } from "immutable";

Range(0, 10)
  .filter(isPrime)
  .forEach(log);

function isPrime(number){ }

function log(number) {
  console.log(number);
}
```

Range(0, 10) generates all numbers from 0 to 9 and then uses `filter` to select all the prime numbers and returns a new sequence containing only those numbers. Then we use `forEach` to display those numbers.

Below we can see how to refactor the loop detecting the prime numbers using the `Range` sequence.

```
import { Range } from 'immutable';

Range(0, 10)
  .filter(isPrime)
  .forEach(log);

function isPrime(number) {
  if (number > 2){
    const firstDivisor = findFirstDivisor(number);
    return !firstDivisor;
  } else {
    return (number === 2)
      ? true
      : false;
  }
}

function findFirstDivisor(number){
  return Range(2, (number / 2) + 1)
    .find(isDivisorOf(number));
}

function isDivisorOf(number) {
  return function(divisor) {
    return (number > 1)
      ? number % divisor === 0
      : false
  };
}

function log(number) { }
```

`isDivisorOf` is a curried function that gets a number and returns a predicate function taking a possible divisor and returning a boolean value.

`findFirstDivisor` returns the first divisor of a number. It checks all numbers from 2 to its half for that.

`isPrime` decides if a number is a prime based on the result of `findFirstDivisor`. If the number has no divisors then it is a prime number.

Recap

Transducers are functions taking a reducer and returning a new reducer.

Lazy sequences like `Seq` allow us to efficiently chain transformation methods without creating intermediate collections.

`Range` provides sequences of numbers.

Chapter 13: Generators

A generator is a function that returns the next value from a sequence each time it is called.

We will start with a simple generator function that gives the next integer each time it is called. It starts from 0.

```
function range() {
  let count = 0;
  return function() {
    const result = count;
    count += 1;
    return result;
  }
}

const nextNumber = range()
console.log(nextNumber()); //0
console.log(nextNumber()); //1
console.log(nextNumber()); //2
```

nextNumber is an infinite generator. nextNumber is a closure with an internal private state.

Finite Generators

Generators can be finite. Check the next example where range creates a generator that returns consecutive numbers from a specific interval. At the end of the sequence, it returns undefined.

```
function range(from, to){
  let count = from;
  return function(){
```

```
    if(count < to){
      const result = count;
      count += 1;
      return result;
    } else {
      return undefined;
    }
  }
}

const nextNumber = range(0, 3)
console.log(nextNumber()); //0
console.log(nextNumber()); //1
console.log(nextNumber()); //2
console.log(nextNumber()); //undefined
```

toArray

When working with generators, we may want to create an array with all the values from the sequence. For this situation, we need a utility function like toArray taking a generator and returning all the values from the sequence as an array. The sequence should be finite.

```
function toArray(generate) {
    let arr = [];
    let value = generate();

    while (value !== undefined) {
        arr = [...arr, value];
        value = generate();
    }
    return arr;
}
```

Let's use it with the previous generator.

```
const numbers = toArray(range(1, 5));
console.log(numbers);
//[1, 2, 3, 4]
```

forEach

We may also need to run a callback for each element in the sequence. The forEach utility function does just that. It gets a generator and a callback and runs the callback until the generator returns undefined.

```
function forEach(callback){
  return function(generate){
    let value = generate();

    while(value !== undefined){
      callback(value);
      value = generate();
    }
  }
}
```

This is a curried function that first takes the callbacks and then the generator.

In the next example, the log function is called for all numbers returned by the generator.

```
function log(x){
  console.log(x);
}

const nextNumber = range(1, 4);
forEach(log)(nextNumber);
//1
//2
//3
```

take

Another common scenario is to take only the first n elements from a sequence. In this case, we need a new utility function like take that receives a generator and creates a new generator returning only the first n elements from the sequence.

```
function take(n) {
  return function(generate) {
    let count = 0;
```

```
    return function() {
      if (count < n) {
        count += 1;
        return generate();
      }
    };
  };
}
```

Again `take` is a curried function and should be called like this: `take(n)(sequence)`.

Here is how you can use `take` and `forEach` in a pipeline to get and log to console the first three values from an infinite sequence of numbers.

```
import { pipe } from 'lodash/fp';

const nextNumber = range();
pipe(
  take(3),
  forEach(console.log)
)(nextNumber);
//0
//1
//2
```

Custom Generators

We can create any custom generator and use it with the previous utility functions. Let's create the Fibonacci custom generator:

```
function fibonacci() {
  let a = 0;
  let b = 1;
  return function() {
    const aResult = a;
    a = b;
    b = aResult + b;
    return aResult;
  };
}
```

We can use the Fibonacci generator with the utility functions already created to display the first 5 numbers in the sequence.

```
import { pipe } from 'lodash/fp';

const generateFibonacci = fibonacci();
pipe(
  take(5),
  forEach(console.log)
)(generateFibonacci);
//0
//1
//1
//2
//3
```

Recap

A generator is a function that returns a new value from a sequence, each time it is called.

Functional generators can return elements from finite or infinite sequences of values.

Chapter 14: Promises

A promise is an object containing a future result.

A promise has three states: pending, fulfilled, and rejected.

- Pending is the initial state of a promise. The result is not available at this stage.
- Fulfilled is the state marking a successful operation. The result is available at this point.
- Rejected is the state marking a failed operation. The result is not available, instead, we have access to the error object giving the details of why the operation failed.

Initially, the promise starts with the pending state. Then it can go to fulfilled or rejected states. Once a promise is fulfilled or rejected, it stays in that state.

Here is a representation of the flow a promise can go through.

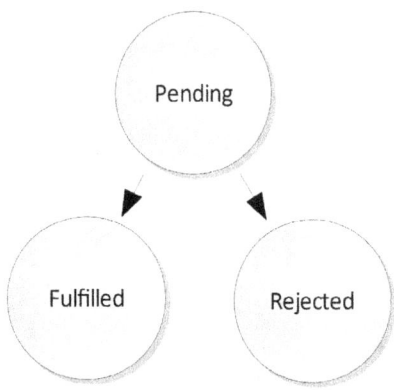

Creating Promises

Let's start by creating a simple promise.

```
function delay(interval){
  return new Promise(function(resolve){
    return setTimeout(resolve, interval);
  });
}

function logDone(){
  console.log('Done');
}

delay(1000)
  .then(logDone);
```

`delay` creates a promise that will resolve in a specific amount of time. We can use it to delay the execution of a task.

Creating a promise with `new Promise` requires passing in a function called the executor function. This function takes two callbacks, `resolve` and `reject`, that can be called later to change the state of the promise. The executor function runs automatically when the promise is created.

`Promise` has two utility static methods, `resolve` and `reject`, to quickly create a resolved or rejected promise.

`Promise.resolve(value)` creates a resolved promise wrapping a `value`.

`Promise.reject(error)` creates a rejected promise.

Success Handling

Mapping

`then` acts as a map. It takes a mapping function and returns a promise containing the transformed value.

We can use a `Promise.resolve` to create a simple mappable object wrapping a value. Then we can transform and inspect the wrapped value.

```
function toUpperCase(text){
  return text.toUpperCase();
}
```

```
function logIdentity(value){
  console.log(value);
  return value;
}

Promise.resolve('sTudY')
  .then(logIdentity)   //"sTudY"
  .then(toUpperCase)
  .then(logIdentity);  //"STUDY"
```

Flat Mapping

then acts also like a flat map.

When the mapping function returns a value, **then** returns a promise containing the transformed value. To be more precise, we should say that the mapping function returns a value that is not a promise.

When the mapping function returns a promise wrapping a value, **then** does not wrap it into another promise. It just returns the new promise containing the transformed value.

Wrapping a promise into another promise would have meant to create a promise which contains a promise which wraps a value.

Take a look at a function, dividing two numbers, that is used as a mapping function on a promise.

```
function devideBy(n, divisor){
  return n / divisor;
}

function logIdentity(value){}

Promise.resolve(9)
  .then(logIdentity)   //9
  .then(n => devideB(n, 3))
  .then(logIdentity);  //3
```

We can implement **devideBy** as a curried function and used it more nicely with **then**.

```
function devideBy(divisor){
```

```
  return function(n){
    return n / divisor;
  }
}
```

```
Promise.resolve(9)
  .then(logIdentity)   //9
  .then(devideBy(3))
  .then(logIdentity); //3
```

When **devideBy** returns a promise instead of number, **then** waits for that promise to complete and returns a promise wrapping the transformed value.

```
function devideBy(divisor){
  return function(number){
    const result = number / divisor;
    return Promise.resolve(result);
  }
}
```

```
Promise.resolve(9)
  .then(logIdentity)   //9
  .then(devideBy(3))
  .then(logIdentity); //3
```

Error Handling

catch handles errors in a promise chain.

Below is an example of error handling using **catch**.

```
function devideBy(divisor){
  return function(number){
    const result = number / divisor;
    return (divisor !== 0)
      ? Promise.resolve(result)
      : Promise.reject("Can't divide by 0")
  }
}

function logError(error){
  console.error(error);
```

```
}

Promise.resolve(9)
  .then(logIdentity) //9
  .then(devideBy(0))
  .then(logIdentity)
  .catch(logError) //"Can't divide by 0"
```

If there is an error in any transformation step the flow jumps down the closest error handler.

Chaining

As you noticed, we can chain several transformations on the wrapped value.

The `then` method on a resolved promise will return a new promise. Likewise, the `catch` method of a rejected promise will return a new promise. This creates a pipeline of transformations where each transform function takes as input the result of the previous one.

```
function toCelsius(kelvin){
  const celsius = (kelvin - 273.15);
  return Math.round(celsius * 100) / 100;
}

function toChangeAction(temperature){
  return {
    type : 'CHANGE_TEMPERATURE',
    temperature
  }
}

function logIdentity(value){}

Promise.resolve(280)
  .then(logIdentity)
  .then(toCelsius)
  .then(logIdentity)
  .then(toChangeAction)
  .then(logIdentity);
  //280
```

```
//6.85
//{ type: 'CHANGE_TEMPERATURE', temperature: 6.85 }
```

`toCelsius` takes the 280-kelvin temperature as input and returns 6.85. `toChangeAction` takes as input the 6.85-celsius temperature and returns an action object containing the new celsius value.

Asynchronous Operations

The code written so far was synchronous. That means we had the result of executing a function immediately.

Consider the next code.

```
const result = Math.pow(2, 3);
console.log(result);
//8
```

One we execute `Math.pow` we have the result.

Now think about what it means to make a call to a Web API and have the returned data in a variable.

```
const result = fetch('/todos')
```

In order to have the data returned by the Web API inside the `result` variable, we need to wait for the fetch call to finish. Waiting means blocking the UI and we don't want that.

Promises offer a solution to this scenario. Instead of returning the result, the fetch call returns a promise that will later give access to the result when it is available.

Parcel

We can test the network call by starting a development server. We can create one using the Parcel web application which requires zero configuration.

First, install Parcel.

```
npm install parcel-bundler --save-dev
```

Next, create an `index.html` and reference the js files you want to check.

```
<html>
<body>
```

```
<script src="./ajax.js"></script>
</body>
</html>
```

Then, add the `dev` task scripts in the `package.json`.

```
{
    "scripts": {
        "dev": "parcel index.html"
    }
}
```

Now, you can start the development server and access the `index.html` page.

Fetch

The Fetch API provides an interface for fetching resources. The `fetch` function takes as input an URL and returns a promise that resolves to the `Response` of the request. It fails when the request fails.

Here is an example of making a fetch call and accessing the result in the returned promise.

```
function toJson(response){
  return response.json();
}

function logIdentity(value){}

function logError(error){
  console.error(error);
}

fetch('https://api.github.com/gists/public')
  .then(toJson)
  .then(logIdentity)
  .catch(logError);
```

The `json()` method converts the response to a JavaScript object. It returns a promise wrapping the result of parsing the response body text as JSON.

Promise.race

Promise.race takes an array of promises and returns the first one that fulfills or rejects.

```
const dictionariesPromise =
  fetch('/dictionaries').then(toJson);

const todosPromise =
  fetch('/todos').then(toJson);

Promise.race([
  dictionariesPromise,
  todosPromise
]).then(logIdentity);
```

Promise.all

Promise.all takes an array of promises and returns a new promise that resolves when all of the input's promises have resolved. If one of the input promises it rejected it rejects immediately.

Promise.all can be used to make sure that all input promises have completed successfully.

```
Promise.all([
  dictionariesPromise,
  todosPromise
]).then(logIdentity);
```

Promise.allSettled

Promise.allSettled takes an array of promises and returns a promise that resolves after all of the input's promises have either fulfilled or rejected. It resolves with an array of objects describing the outcome of each promise.

```
const dictionariesPromise =
  fetch('/dictionaries').then(toJson);
const todosPromise =
  fetch('/todos').then(toJson);
const rejectedPromise = Promise.reject('Error');

Promise.allSettled([
```

```
  dictionariesPromise,
  todosPromise,
  rejectedPromise
])
  .then(logIdentity)
  //[
  //{status: "fulfilled", value: Array(1)},
  //{status: "fulfilled", value: Array(1)},
  //{status: "rejected", reason: "Error"}
  //]
```

Functor Laws

The `then` method on a promise acts as a `map` when the transformation function returns an object that is not a promise.

Let's check the functor laws.

We require a constructor function that creates a promise from a value. We don't need to define such a function because we can use existing helpers like `Promise.resolve` that can make a promise from a value.

When building a promise with `Promise.resolve`, `M(x)` translates to `Promise.resolve(x)`.

Identity law is respected.

```
function identity(n){
  return n;
}

Promise.resolve(1)
  .then(identity)
  //Promise 1
```

The composition law is respected when mapping functions don't return promises. In this case, `promise.then(f).then(g)` gives the same result as `promise.then(x => g(f(x)))`.

```
function f(x){
  return x + 1;
}

function g(x){
```

```
    return x * 2;
}

Promise.resolve(1)
   .then(f)
   .then(g)
   //Promise 4

Promise.resolve(1)
   .then(x => g(f(x)))
   //Promise 4
```

The functor composition law is broken when one transformation function returns a promise and the other doesn't. Here is an example.

```
function f(x){
   return Promise.resolve(x + 1);
}

function g(x){
   return x * 2;
}

Promise.resolve(1)
   .then(f)
   .then(g)
   //Promise 4

Promise.resolve(1)
   .then(x => g(f(x)))
   //Promise NaN
```

In this case, the promise does not work as a functor because it doesn't respect the composition law. In practical terms, we should not refactor

```
promise
   .then(f)
   .then(g)
```

to

```
promise
   .then(x => g(f(x)))
```

Monad Laws

The `then` method on a promise acts like `flatMap` when the transformation function returns a promise.

Calling `then` with a transformation function creating a promise, returns a new promise wrapping a value. It does not return a promise, containing a promise, wrapping a value.

The left identity is respected when the wrapped value is not a promise itself.

```
//M(x).flatMap(f) === f(x)

function f(x){
  return Promise.resolve(x + 1);
}

Promise.resolve(1)
  .then(f)
  //Promise 2

f(1)
  //Promise 2
```

When the wrapped value is a promise the left identity is broken.

```
function f(p){
  return p.then(n => n + 1);
}

const x = Promise.resolve(1);

Promise.resolve(x)
  .then(f));
  //TypeError: p.then is not a function

f(x)
  //Promise 2
```

The right identity is confirmed.

```
// M(x).flatMap(M) === M(x)
```

```
function M(value){
  return Promise.resolve(value)
}

M(1).then(M)
  //Promise 1

M(1)
  //Promise 1
```

Associativity is satisfied only if f and g do not take a promise argument.

In that case `promise.flatMap(f).flatMap(g)` gives the same result as `promise.flatMap(x => f(x).flatMap(g))`.

```
function f(x){
  return Promise.resolve(x + 1);
}

function g(x){
  return Promise.resolve(x * 2);
}

Promise.resolve(1)
  .then(f)
  .then(g)
  //Promise 4

Promise.resolve(1)
  .then(x => f(x).then(g))
  //Promise 4
```

When f or g take a promise argument the law is not respected failing like in the left identity check.

As we have seen the functor composition law is broken when one transformation function returns a promise and the other does not. The left identity and associativity monad laws are not respected for every mapping function taking a value and returning a promise. They are satisfied only when the input value for those mapping functions is not a promise itself.

Failing to satisfy one law is enough to disqualify an object supporting mapping and flat mapping from being a monad. Several laws are broken so promises are not monads, not functors.

Recap

Promises are objects wrapping a future result.

When the transformation function returns a value, `then` acts as a `map` operation. When it returns another promise, `then` acts like a `flatMap` operation.

Promises do not obey the functor and monad laws so they are not monads even if they behave similarly to them in specific cases.

Chapter 15: Observables

An observable is a stream of data that can arrive over time. Observable are objects emitting values to listeners as these values become available.

Observables may become part of the JavaScript language in the future, but for the time being, we are going to use the implementation of observables from the RxJS library.

```
npm install rxjs --save
```

Operators are a powerful feature available on observables.

Creation Operators

Creation operators are functions used to construct new observables.

Observables are commonly created using creation functions, like `of`, `from`, `interval` or `ajax`.

create()

The following example creates an observable that emits the values 1, 2, 3 to subscribers and then completes.

```
import { Observable } from 'rxjs';

const observable = Observable.create(observer => {
  observer.next(1);
  observer.next(2);
  observer.next(3);
  observer.complete();
});
```

The `create` operator takes a callback function defining how to emit values. There are three methods describing what an observable can do.

- `next()` sends a value to listeners.
- `error()` sends an error to listeners.
- `complete()` marks the end of the sequence of values. After calling `complete`, further calls to `next()` have no effect.

`next` defines the actual data being delivered to a subscriber. The data flow may either complete with success using `complete` or fail marked using `error`.

We can listen to the observable source using the `subscribe` method.

```
observable
  .subscribe(console.log);
//1
//2
//3
```

If we subscribe again later to the source of data we receive again all the emitted values.

```
setTimeout(()=>{
  observable.subscribe(console.log);
  //1
  //2
  //3
}, 3000);
```

of()

of creates observables from a set of values. Here is an example of an observable that emits 1, 2, 3 in order.

```
import { of } from 'rxjs';

const source = of(1, 2, 3);
source
  .subscribe(console.log);
// 1
// 2
// 3
```

from()

`from` can create observables from an array-like object, a promise, or an observable-like object.

Here is an example of building an observable from an array.

```
import { from } from 'rxjs';

const observable = from([1, 2, 3]);
observable.subscribe(console.log);
// 1
// 2
// 3
```

interval()

The `interval` function takes the n number of milliseconds as input and returns an observable emitting a new integer in order every n milliseconds.

```
import { interval } from 'rxjs';

const observable = interval(1000);
observable.subscribe(console.log);
//0 -> after 1s
//1 -> after 2s
//2 -> after 3s
//3 -> after 4s
//4 -> after 5s
//5 -> after 6s
```

ajax()

`ajax` creates an observable getting the result from a network request. It takes as input either a request object with the URL, method, data, etc, or a just an URL string.

Here is an example.

```
import { ajax } from 'rxjs/ajax';

ajax('https://api.github.com/gists/public')
   .subscribe(console.log);
```

The observable stream created with the `ajax` function emits the response object returned from the request.

Below the same request is done with the `ajax.getJSON` function creating an observable that emits only the JSON key of the response object returned from the request.

```
ajax.getJSON('https://api.github.com/gists/public')
  .subscribe(console.log);
```

Pipeable Operators

Observables have the `pipe` method that allows pipelining multiple operators.

Pipeable operators are those operators that can be piped to observables using the pipe syntax. These include operators like `filter`, `map`, or `take`.

A pipeable operator is a function that takes an observable as input and returns another observable. Subscribing to the output observable will also subscribe to the input observable.

Operators transform the values from the stream of data. They return an observable of the transformed values.

`map` transforms values from an observable source using a mapping function.

```
import { of } from 'rxjs';
import { map } from 'rxjs/operators';

const dataSource = of(1, 2, 3);

function double(n){
    return n * 2;
}

dataSource
  .pipe(
    map(double)
  )
  .subscribe(console.log);
  //2
  //4
  //6
```

`filter` filters the stream values using a predicate function.

```
import { of } from 'rxjs';
import { map, filter } from 'rxjs/operators';

const dataSource = of(1, 2, 3, 4, 5);

function isEven(n){
  return n % 2 === 0;
}

dataSource
  .pipe(
    filter(isEven)
  )
  .subscribe(console.log);
  //2
  //4
```

The `take` operator allows selecting only the first n emitted values from an observable source. Below is an example of selecting the first three values from the source.

```
import { of } from 'rxjs';
import { take } from 'rxjs/operators';

const source = of(1, 2, 3, 4, 5);
source
  .pipe(
    take(3)
  )
  .subscribe(console.log);
  //1
  //2
  //3
```

The `pipe` method creates a pipeline on the observable source. It allows us to pass the data through a pipeline of operators transforming it.

```
import { of } from 'rxjs';
import { map, filter } from 'rxjs/operators';

const dataSource = of(1, 2, 3, 4, 5);
```

```
function isEven(n){
  return n % 2 === 0;
}

function double(n){
  return n * 2;
}

dataSource
  .pipe(
    filter(isEven),
    map(double)
  )
  .subscribe(console.log);
//4
//8
```

Observers

Observers are objects having three callbacks, one for each type of notification delivered by the observable. Observers are the consumer of values delivered by observables.

Here is a simple observer object handling all types of notifications.

```
const observer = {
  next(value){
    console.log(`Next: ${value}`)
  },
  error(msg){
    console.error(`Error: ${msg}`)
  },
  complete(value){
    console.error(`Complete`)
  }
};
```

The observer is used as an argument to the subscribe method of an observable.

```
const observable = Observable.create(observer => {
    observer.next(1);
```

```
    observer.next(2);
    observer.complete('Done');
});
observable.subscribe(observer);
//Next: 1
//Next: 2
//Complete
```

Below is an example of subscribing to an observable that emits two values and then fails.

```
const observable = Observable.create(observer => {
  observer.next(1);
  observer.next(2);
  observer.error('Failed');
});

observable.subscribe(observer);
//Next: 1
//Next: 2
//Error: Failed
```

There is no need to have a callback in the observer object for all notification types. Some notifications can be ignored.

We can subscribe to an observable by just providing a callback as an argument and not an observer object. This is equivalent to creating an observer with just the `next` handler.

```
observable.subscribe(value => console.log(`Next: ${value}`));
```

All three types of callbacks can be provided as arguments to the `subscribe` method. This is equivalent to creating an observer with all three handlers.

```
observable.subscribe(
  value => console.log(`Next: ${value}`),
  msg => console.error(`Error: ${msg}`),
  () => console.error(`Complete`)
);
```

Subscriptions

A subscription is an object created when subscribing to an observable. It allows us to `unsubscribe` form that observable.

```
import { interval } from 'rxjs';

const observable = interval(1000);
const subscription = observable.subscribe(console.log);

//later
setTimeout(() => {
  subscription.unsubscribe();
}, 3500);
//0 -> after 1s
//1 -> after 2s
//2 -> after 3s
```

The subscription object has just the **unsubscribe** method. When all subscribers unsubscribe from an observable, that observable stops its execution.

An observable starts its execution when it has at least one subscriber.

Higher-Order Observables

In most cases, observables emit primitives or data objects but sometimes they may emit other observables. In this case, they are called higher-order observables.

Consider for example an observables emitting URL strings. We may have a mapping function taking the URL and returning a new observable.

```
import { from } from 'rxjs';
import { ajax } from 'rxjs/ajax';
import { map } from 'rxjs/operators';

const observable = from([
  '/dictionaries',
  '/todos'
]);

observable.pipe(
  map(ajax.getJSON)
).subscribe(console.log);
//Observable {}
//Observable {}
```

`ajax.getJSON` is the mapping function. It takes the URL and returns an observable emitting the response from the network request for each URL. After this transformation, we have an observable of observables, a higher-order observable.

The challenge is to work with a higher-order observable. In this case, we need a flattening operation, meaning we need to convert the higher-order observable into an ordinary observable.

Flattening Operators

Instead of working with an observable that emits observables wrapping the data got from the server, we want to work with an observable emitting the data got from the server.

concatAll()

The `concatAll` operator subscribes to each observable inside the "outer" observable and copies all the emitted values until that inner observable completes. Then it goes to the next one. It creates a new observable emitting all these concatenated values.

Here is how we can use it to flatten the higher-order observable and get an observable emitting the results of all network requests.

```
import { from } from 'rxjs';
import { ajax } from 'rxjs/ajax';
import { map, concatAll } from 'rxjs/operators';

const observable = from([
    '/dictionaries',
    '/todos'
]);

observable.pipe(
    map(ajax.getJSON),
    concatAll()
).subscribe(console.log);
//[{name: 'Dictionary'}]
//[{title: 'To Do'}]
```

mergeAll()

Another useful flattening is `mergeAll`. It subscribes to each inner observable as it arrives, then emits each value as it arrives.

Using `mergeAll` instead of `concatAll` in the previous example makes no difference because each of the inner AJAX observable emits just a single value. The difference can be seen when the inner observables emit several values over time.

mergeMap()

Consider a mapping function that takes a value and returns an observable emitting the first three numbers from a sequence. The sequence of numbers is defined using the input value as the `c` constant and applying the `n*c + 1` formula.

When `c = 2` the sequence formula is `2n + 1` and the first three values are 3, 5 and 7.

When `c = 4` the sequence formula is `4n + 1` and the first three values are 5, 9 and 13.

Here is the `toSequence` mapping function creating an observable.

```
function toSequence(x) {
  const getNTerm = createGetNTerm(x);
  return of(1, 2, 3).pipe(
    map(getNTerm)
  )
}

function createGetNTerm(c){
  return function(n){
    return n * c + 1
  }
}
```

When invoked with the value 2, `toSequence` returns an observable emitting 3, 5 and 7.

```
toSequence(2)
//Observable 3 5 7

toSequence(4)
```

```
//Observable 5 9 13
```

Next, let's apply the `toSequence` mapping function to an observable containing several values that are to be used as constants in the newly created sequences.

```
import { from } from 'rxjs';
import { map, mergeAll } from 'rxjs/operators';

from([2, 4]).pipe(
    map(toSequence)
  )
  .subscribe(console.log);
  //Observable 3 5 7
  //Observable 5 9 13
```

At this point, we have an observable emitting observables containing the first three numbers from the sequence.

Using `mergeAll` will create a new observable emitting the numbers from all generated sequences. First, it emits all the numbers from the first sequence, then from the second and so on.

```
from([2, 4]).pipe(
    map(toSequence),
    mergeAll()
  )
  //.subscribe(console.log);
  //3
  //5
  //7
  //5
  //9
  //13
```

`mergeMap` does the same thing as applying `map` and then calling `mergeAll`.

```
from([2, 4]).pipe(
    mergeMap(toSequence)
  )
  .subscribe(console.log);
  //3
  //5
  //7
```

```
//5
//9
//13
```

Combining Observables

Next, we are going to look at operators for combining multiple observables into a single one.

forkJoin()

Let's take the situation of two observables emitting results from network requests. We want to execute logic when both network requests have completed.

```
import { ajax } from 'rxjs/ajax';
import { forkJoin } from 'rxjs';

const dictionariesObservable = ajax.getJSON('/dictionaries');
const todosObservable = ajax.getJSON('/todos');

forkJoin({
    dictionaries: dictionariesObservable,
    todos: todosObservable
}).subscribe(console.log);
//{dictionaries: Array(), todos: Array()}
```

`forkJoin` creates an observable from other observables. When all inner observables complete, it provides the last emitted value from each as a dictionary.

The `forkJoin` operator allows us to issue multiple requests on the page loaded and take action when a response has been received from all. It is similar to `Promise.all`.

race()

`race` takes several observables and returns the observable that emits first. It is similar to `Promise.race`.

```
import { ajax } from 'rxjs/ajax';
import { race } from 'rxjs';
```

```
const dictionariesObservable =
  ajax.getJSON('/dictionaries');
const todosObservable =
  ajax.getJSON('/todos');

const observable = race(
  dictionariesObservable,
  todosObservable
);

observable.subscribe(console.log);
```

Functor Laws

Observables have a map operation that respects both functor laws.

Identity Law

```
import { of } from 'rxjs';
import { map } from 'rxjs/operators';

function identity(n){
    return n;
}

of(1, 2, 3)
  .pipe(
    map(identity)
  )
  //Observable 1,2,3
```

Composition Law

```
import { of } from 'rxjs';
import { map } from 'rxjs/operators';

function increment(n){
  return n + 1;
}

function double(n){
  return n * 2
}
```

```
of(1, 2, 3)
  .pipe(
    map(increment),
    map(double)
  )
  //Observable 4,6,8

of(1, 2, 3)
  .pipe(
    map(x => double(increment(x)))
  )
  //Observable 4,6,8
```

Observables are functors.

Monad Laws

Observables have a flat mapping operation called **mergeMap** that respects the monad laws.

Left Identity

`M.unit(x).flatMap(f) === f(x)`

We can consider `of` as the unit function creating an observable.

```
import { of } from 'rxjs';
import { mergeMap } from 'rxjs/operators';

function f(n){
  return of(n + 1);
}

of(1)
  .pipe(
    mergeMap(f)
  )
  //Observable 2

f(1)
  //Observable 2
```

Right Identity

Applying the unit function to an observable results in an observable emitting the same values.

```
function unit(value){
  return of(value)
}

of(1)
  .pipe(
    mergeMap(unit)
  )
  .subscribe(console.log);
  //Observable 1
```

Associativity

```
monad.flatMap(f).flatMap(g)
  === monad.flatMap(x => f(x).flatMap(g)))
```

Here is how we can translate the law for observables.

```
function g(n){
  return of(n * 2);
}

of(1)
  .pipe(
    mergeMap(f),
    mergeMap(g)
  )
  //Observable 4

of(1)
  .pipe(
    mergeMap(x => f(x).pipe(mergeMap(g)))
  )
  //Observable 4
```

Observables are monads.

Recap

Observables are streams of data. The consumers of these observables are the observers subscribing to those streams.

Creation functions like `of`, `from`, `interval` or `ajax` make new observables.

Observables offer a solution for doing asynchronous tasks, plus they have a set of powerful operators for processing the results. Pipeable operators like `filter`, `map`, or `take` get an observable as input and return another observable emitting the transformed values.

Observables emitting other observables are called higher-order observables. Flattening operations like `concatAll`, `mergeAll`, `mergeMap` allow us to convert higher-order observables into ordinary observables.

Chapter 16: Elm Architecture

Next, we are going to learn how to create a simple application in a functional style by building one using the Elm purely functional language. Then we will implement the same functionality with React and Redux. The point is to understand the architecture that supports this style of programming.

Start by creating the Elm project. Navigate to a new folder and create the Elm project by running:

`elm init`

The command creates an `elm.json` file and a `src` folder for all Elm files.

`elm reactor` opens the development server. It starts a server at `http://localhost:8000`. From there we can navigate to any Elm file.

Elm Architecture

The Elm Architecture defines the data flow inside an Elm application. It breaks the application into the following core parts:

- Model - defines all the state of the application.
- View - is a pure function that transforms the state data into HTML. The HTML sends back messages.
- Messages - expresses the user interaction.
- Update - is a pure function returning a new state based on the current message and the actual state.

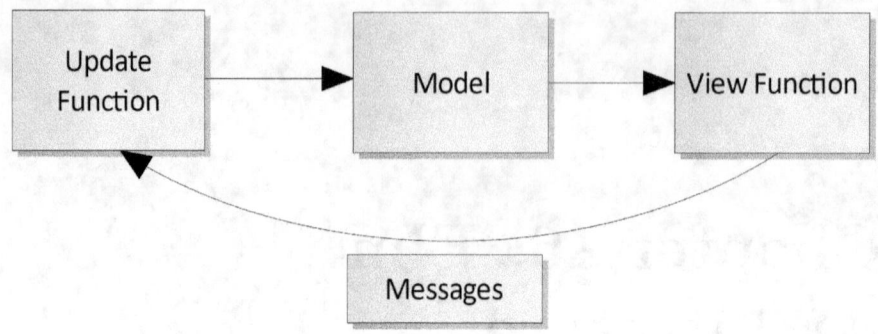

In the next examples, we are going to use this architectural pattern to create a few functionalities.

Counter with Elm

Let's implement a simple counter page and discuss the Elm Architecture.

Model

The model stores all the application data that can change. In our case, we just need to store a number to reflect the current count.

The initial value of this counter is 0.

```
type alias Model = {
    number : Int
  }

initialModel : Model
initialModel = { number = 0 }
```

Messages

Messages define user interaction. The user can increase or decrease the count so we need two messages to express those actions.

```
type Msg = Increment | Decrement
```

View Function

The `view` function takes in the `Model` as an argument and displays it on the screen. The view function creates the HTML.

The HTML contains a decrement button that generates the `Decrement` message, and an increment button that generates the `Increment` message and the current count. The count number is read from the model, converted to a string, and then rendered as text inside a `div` element.

Messages are generated by handling the `onClick` event for each button.

```
view : Model -> Html Msg
view model =
  div []
    [
      div [] [ text (String.fromInt model.number) ]
    , button [ onClick Decrement ] [ text "-" ]
    , button [ onClick Increment ] [ text "+" ]
    ]
```

Update Function

The `update` function describes how to change the model when receiving a new message.

When it gets the `Increment` message, it returns a new model with the number incremented. When it gets the `Decrement` message, it returns a new model with the number decremented.

```
update : Msg -> Model -> Model
update msg model =
  case msg of
    Increment ->
      { model | number = model.number + 1 }

    Decrement ->
      { model | number = model.number - 1 }
```

The initial number is zero and it increases and decreases when the user presses different buttons.

Wiring-Up

The `main` value describes what it is shown on the screen. It needs the initial model, the `view` function to generate the HTML, and `update` function to change the model.

```
import Browser
```

```
import Html exposing (Html, button, div, text)
import Html.Events exposing (onClick)

//Code

main =
  Browser.sandbox {
    init = initialModel,
    update = update,
    view = view
  }
```

The `view` function takes the initial model and displays on the screen. The user actions generate messages. The `update` handles those action and updates the model. When the model is changed the `view` function is called to render the new model on screen. This flow repeats endlessly.

Counter with React and Redux

Now let's implement the same counter page in JavaScript with React and Redux.

Model

The model defines all the application data. We can define the counter as the `number` property on the application state object.

```
const initialModel = {
  number: 0
};
```

Messages

The two messages for increasing and decreasing the count can be expressed as functions creating plain data object having the `type` property.

```
function Increment(){
  return {
    type : Increment.name
  }
}

function Decrement(){
```

```
    return {
      type : Decrement.name
    }
}

export { Increment, Decrement };
```

View Function

The view function can be implemented using React functional components. These components return an HTML-like syntax called JSX.

```
import React from 'react';
import { connect } from 'react-redux';
import { Increment, Decrement } from './store';

function Counter({number, Increment, Decrement}){
  return(
    <div>
      <div>{number}</div>
        <button
         type="button"
         onClick={Decrement}>-</button>
        <button
         type="button"
         onClick={Increment}>+</button>
    </div>
  )
}

export default connect(
 state => state,
 {Increment, Decrement}
)(Counter);
```

Update Function

The update function takes the current model and message and returns the new model.

```
function reducer(model = initialModel, action){
  switch(action.type){
```

```
      case Increment.name:
        return { ...model, number: model.number + 1 };
      case Decrement.name:
        return { ...model, number: model.number - 1 };
      default:
        return model;
  }
}

export { reducer };
```

Wiring-Up

We can wire up all these in the application entry point file `index.js`. Here we specify the initial state, the view, and the update functions.

```
import React from 'react';
import ReactDOM from 'react-dom';
import { createStore } from 'redux';
import { Provider } from 'react-redux';
import Counter from './Counter';
import { reducer } from './store';

const store = createStore(reducer);

ReactDOM.render(
  <React.StrictMode>
    <Provider store={store}>
      <Counter />
    </Provider>
  </React.StrictMode>,
  document.getElementById('root')
);
```

Random Number with Elm

Next, we will create another page that displays a random number. This may look simpler than previous functionality but it is actually harder to do because generating random numbers cannot be done with a pure function.

Pure functions are deterministic functions. Called with the same input they always return the same output. Elm is a purely functional language. That means it allows us to write only pure functions. How is possible then to generate random numbers and write only pure functions?

Let's find out.

Model

Again we need a model to store our application data that can change. The model contains just a number.

```
type alias Model = {
    number : Int
  }

initModel : () -> (Model, Cmd Msg)
initModel _ =
  ( Model 0
  , Cmd.none
  )
```

Messages

The user can press the generate button so we need a message to express that interaction, `GenerateNumber`.

```
type Msg = GenerateNumber
```

View

The view function takes the model and renders the UI. It displays the current number stored in the model inside a `div` element. It also shows the button for generating a new number. When the button is pressed the `GenerateNumber` message is created.

```
view : Model -> Html Msg
view model =
  div []
    [
      div [] [ text (String.fromInt model.number) ]
    , button [ onClick GenerateNumber ] [ text "Generate" ]
    ]
```

Update

The update function takes the current messages and generates the new model. The update function is pure. It cannot generate a random number. Instead what it does is to create a command telling the Elm framework to generate the random number and then put the result inside a new message. We are going to call this new message `SetNumber`. At this point we realize that messages can take arguments, messages can be functions.

```
type Msg = GenerateNumber | SetNumber Int
```

In order to use the `Random.generate` command we need to install an additional package.

```
elm install elm/random
```

Here is the update function handling both messages.

```
update : Msg -> Model -> (Model, Cmd Msg)
update msg model =
  case msg of
    GenerateNumber ->
      ( model
      , Random.generate SetNumber (Random.int 1 100)
      )

    SetNumber number ->
      ( Model number
      , Cmd.none
      )
```

When the update function receives the `GenerateNumber` message, it creates a command using the `Random.generate` function. The Elm framework runs the command, generates the random number, and builds a new message `SetNumber` containing this random number. The update function does not modify the model in this case, it returns the same model.

When the update function receives the `SetNumber` messages with the random number it returns a new model containing the newly generated number. The update function does not generate any command in this case, it returns `Cmd.none`.

As noticed in order to work with impure logic the update function returns two things for each message, the new model and a new command that the Elm framework has to execute.

Here is how we can write a function that returns two values in JavaScript. We simply return an array containing the two values. Then we use the destructuring assignment syntax on the left-hand side of the assignment to unpack the returned values.

```
function update(model, action){
  switch(action.type){
    case 'GenerateNumber' : {
      const command = {
        name: 'Random.generate',
        resultMessage : 'SetNumber'
      };
      return [model, command];
    }
    case 'SetNumber' : {
      const newModel = { ...model, number: action.payload };
      const command = { name: 'Cmd.none' };
      return [newModel, command];
    }
    default : {
      const command = { name: 'Cmd.none' };
      return [model, command];
    }
  }
}

const [model, command] = update({}, 'GenerateNumber');
console.log(model);
console.log(command);
//{}
//{name: "Cmd.none"}
```

Note that a command is a plain object describing the command to execute. Also, remark that we use curly brackets inside the switch branches to define a block scope for each clause and allow declaring variables with the same name in different branches.

Below is how the data flow looks like when using commands for handling impure logic.

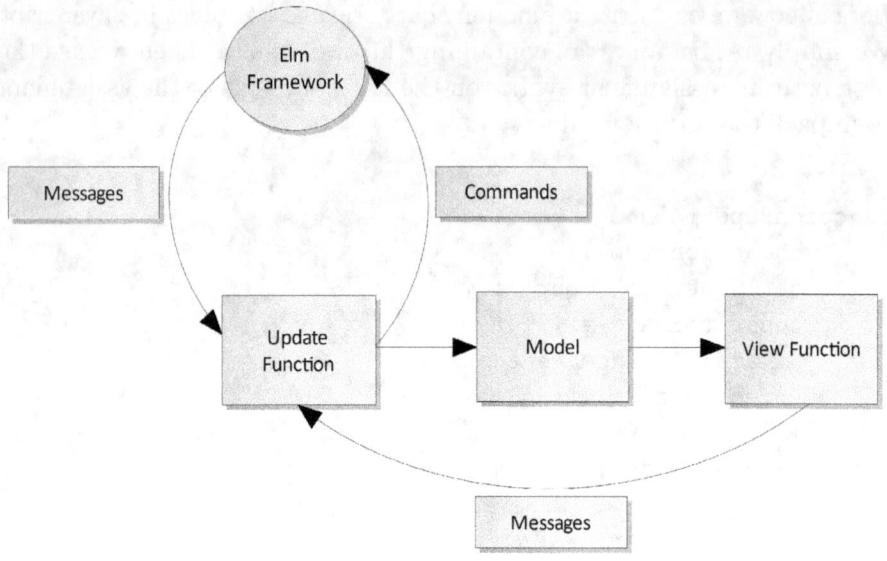

Random Number with React and Redux

Now let's implement the same functionality in JavaScript.

Model

We start by defining the model as an object with the **number** property set to 0.

```
const initialModel = {
  number: 0
};
```

Commands

This is the point where we have problems generating random numbers and still using pure functions. Redux allows us to define a place where to put such impure logic but has no solution to avoid it altogether.

We are going to follow the Redux pattern and define **GenerateNumber** as function returning another function. The returned function is called a thunk and contains the impure logic. The result of this impure logic will be passed as an argument to the **SetNumber** message.

```
function GenerateNumber(){
  return function(dispatch){
```

```
    const number = Math.floor(Math.random() * 100);
    dispatch(SetNumber(number));
  }
}
```

Messages

The `SetNumber` message is needed by the `GenerateNumber` command to send the newly generated number.

```
function SetNumber(number){
  return {
    type : SetNumber.name,
    number
  }
}
```

View

The view function takes the model and creates the HTML for it. When the generate button is pressed it dispatches the `GenerateNumber` command.

```
import React from 'react';
import { connect } from 'react-redux';
import { GenerateNumber } from './store';

function Counter({number, GenerateNumber}){
  return(
    <div>
      <div>{number}</div>
      <button
        type="button"
        onClick={GenerateNumber}>Generate</button>
    </div>
  )
}

export default connect(
  state => state,
  { GenerateNumber }
)(Counter)
```

Update

The update function handles the application messages. When the `SetNumber` message is received it returns a model with the new number value.

```
function reducer(model = initialModel, action){
  switch(action.type){
    case SetNumber.name:
      return { ...model, number: action.number };
    default:
      return model;
  }
}
```

Recap

The Elm architecture defines the flow that allows us to write a practical application in a functional style.

The model is an immutable object representing all the application state.

The view function is a pure function building the HTML and creating messages. The view function is not responsible for rendering HTML on a screen. It takes a model and returns HTML. The Elm framework uses the view function to render this HTML on the screen.

Messages are requests to modify the application's model.

The update function is a pure function taking in the current model and a message and returning the new model. When dealing with side-effects it also returns a new command. The update function doesn't effectively change the model. The Elm framework uses the update function to change the model. The Elm framework executes the command returned by the update function and creates a new message with the result.

Chapter 17: Functional Paradigm

Now we are going to look back at what it means to program in a functional style.

The main idea in functional programming is to split the application into small pure functions that communicate using immutable data and then compose these functions to implement the required functionality.

Ideally, all the functions in the application should be pure functions.

Purity

As repeated many times, the point of functional programming is to write pure functions. These are functions that just transform values.

When a pure function returns the application has the same state as when the function was called. An application is much easier to understand when we don't have to track variables changing their values. Pure functions make code easier to follow by allowing us to focus our attention in one place.

The challenge is, of course, to create a practical application doing only transformations with pure functions. Is that even possible?

We saw that it is achievable if we have the right framework using these pure functions and doing the impure logic necessary for a practical application. Such architecture was implemented in Elm.

Here is the flow of executing impure logic in Elm:

- The pure update function creates a command describing the impure logic

- The Elm framework takes the command, runs the impure logic and generates a message containing the result
- The pure update function handles this message by creating a new updated model holding the previous result

This kind of approach requires having functions to create commands for any kind of impure logic and using a framework able to understand those commands.

Next, we are going to look at a similar approach for making a fetch call with React and Redux using only pure functions. The fetch call itself is a side-effect, so invoking it in a function makes that function impure.

Luckily for us, there is a Redux middleware, called Axios middleware that can intercept fetch messages, do the fetch call, and then put the result in a new success message.

Let's look at the parts required to implement this functionality.

The model initially stores just an empty list of to-dos.

```
const initialModel = {
  todos: []
};
```

The message object describing the fetch request is created using the LoadTodos pure function.

```
function LoadTodos(){
  return {
    type: LoadTodos.name,
    payload: {
      request:{
        url:'/todos'
      }
    }
  }
}
```

The List view function is pure. It takes the list of todos and creates an HTML. It creates a refresh button that sends LoadTodos messages on clicks.

```
import React from 'react';
import { connect } from 'react-redux';
```

```
import { LoadTodos } from './store';

function List({todos, LoadTodos}){
  return(
    <div>
      <button
        type="button"
        onClick={LoadTodos}>
          Refresh
      </button>
      { todos.map(todo =>
          <div>{todo.title}</div> )}
    </div>
  )
}

export default connect(
  state => state,
  { LoadTodos }
)(List);
```

The update function is pure. It takes the current model and action and returns the new model. When receiving the success message it returns a new model with the new list of to-dos.

```
function reducer(model = initialModel, action){
  switch(action.type){
    case `${LoadTodos.name}_SUCCESS`:
      return {
        ...model,
        todos: action.payload.data
      };
    default:
      return model;
  }
}
```

That's it. We manage to make make a fetch call and display the results on the screen using only pure functions. We can do it because we have at our disposal a set of libraries that handle the impure logic.

Note the data flow in this application:

- clicking on the refresh button creates a message describing a fetch request
- the Axios middleware intercepts the message, makes the fetch call and creates a new success message with the result
- the update function handles the success message by creating a new model with the previous result

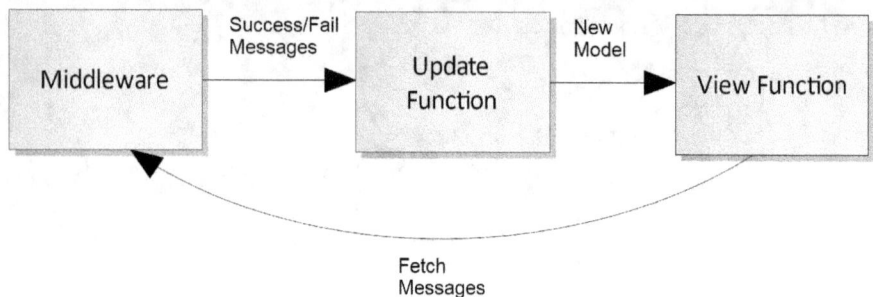

When you think about, this logic for retrieving data has three impure parts:

- fetching the data from a Web API
- updating the model object
- rendering the data on the screen

The Redux-Axios middleware enabled us to make fetch requests using pure functions creating fetch commands. Redux offers a solution to update the model using pure functions. React gives a solution to update the UI using pure view functions. It helps but these are not the only kinds of impure logic we can write. There are many more like coordinating several network requests, creating timer events, generating random numbers, getting the current time, writing to the console or to the local storage, and so on. We call them side-effects.

In JavaScript at the moment of writing the best libraries for writing applications in a functional style, React and Redux, still require to write impure logic. In this case, we need to aim for a high percentage of pure functions. 80% is much better than 20%.

Immutability

It turns out that immutability is much easier to achieve. We can simply freeze objects at creation and they become immutable. Another simple solution is to use a linter to make sure no mutations are done in the application.

Immutable data structures are available in libraries like Immutable.JS. They offer optimization improvements and a nicer public interface.

We should not be concerned about creating intermediate collections when processing a list. When the list is small, less than a thousand records the difference is indistinguishable. When working with collections of thousands of objects we can start using sequences that do not create intermediate collections.

Pipelines

We saw different ways of creating pipelines of data transformations from the `pipe` utility to the chaining transformations on arrays, immutable lists, sequences, promises, or observables.

All these data structures wrap one or more values and allow us the create pipelines of pure functions transforming the wrapped data. Usually, there are a set of common transformations like `filter`, `map`, `reduce`, or `sort` that all these data structures support.

The currying technique is useful in this case to pass additional arguments to the functions in the pipeline.

Functional programming starts to be about transforming data with pipelines of pure functions. In a sense, functional programming promotes a data-flow programming style.

Loops

Purely functional languages do not have loops. Such functionalities are implemented using the array methods and falling back to recursion for specific algorithms.

At the moment of writing it is not possible to disable all loop statements in JavaScript because it lacks the tail-call implementation.

Naming

Splitting the application into pure functions is not enough. We need to give intention revealing names to those functions. So take your time to do that. If you failed the application will still be harder to understand.

Folder Structure

As the application grows more and more functions will be created. You will need to find a way to structure these functions in modules. That means creating files with a clear name containing those functions. Then you need a way to structure those files in folders. There will be common functions and there will be functions used only in a specific module.

Final Thoughts

An application written in a functional style consists of numerous pure functions, organized into modules. We use these functions into pipelines and compose them to implement the required functionalities

Functional programing makes code easier to read. Programs that are not easily understood may lead to bugs and are most often remade.

The essence of functional programming is transforming immutable data using pure functions. These transformations become more expressive in pipelines.

What's next?

'JavaScript: The Fundamentals' book looks at the essential concepts in the JavaScript language. It covers the basic units like numbers, strings, booleans, objects, functions, arrays, sets, maps, dates and regular expressions. It ends by summing up all the core features of JavaScript that make it unique in a sense.

For a more in-depth look at JavaScript and main functional principles, you may read 'Discover Functional JavaScript'. Here, you will find more on pure functions, immutability, currying, decorators but also ideas on how to make code easier to read. JavaScript brings functional programming to the mainstream and offers a new way of doing object-oriented programming without classes and prototypes.

If you want to learn how to build modern React applications using functional components and functional programming principles, you can consider reading 'Functional React, 2nd Edition'.

Continue your learning path with 'Functional Architecture with React and Redux' book, and put in practice what you learned by building several applications with an incremental level of complexity.

The functional architecture implies getting the initial state, showing it to the user using the view functions, listening for actions, updating the state based on those actions, and rendering the updated state back to the user again.

The 'Microblog React Project' book takes a project-based learning approach by engaging you in building a practical application. The reader will learn things on the way by developing different parts of this project. The Microblog application will be built using React with Hooks and libraries like Redux, Redux Thunk, Redux Toolkit, Material UI, or Axios.

The 'UI State Management' book gives you an overview of how state is managed by building a note-taking application with four different libraries. We start from an object-oriented approach using Svelte, centralize state with Vuex, then move to a functional approach with React and Redux, and in the end arrive at a solution using only pure functions with Elm.

The Composition API provides a new way of managing reactivity. It is made of a set of Reactive API functions plus the facility to register lifecycle hooks. Understand better the reactivity system by building one from scratch and then implement a master-details functionality. Check how to manage state using the Composition API and then use it to implement a central store similar to Vuex.

The Principles of Design Patterns help you to write code that is flexible, reusable and easier to maintain. These principles are:

- Program to an interface, not an implementation
- Favor object composition over class inheritance
- Encapsulate the concept that varies

Interfaces enable polymorphic behavior. Factories hide the complexities of creating objects.

Enjoy the learning journey!

About the author

Cristian Salcescu is the author of Discover Functional JavaScript. He is a technical lead passionate about front-end development and enthusiastic about sharing ideas. He took different roles and participated in all parts of software creation.
Cristian Salcescu is a JavaScript trainer and a writer on Medium.

www.ingramcontent.com/pod-product-compliance
Lightning Source LLC
Chambersburg PA
CBHW071405210526
45465CB00001B/252